K. S. Soother
Hull
August 1990

THE LEON VALLEY
Three Herefordshire Villages

To the memory of my old friend
Frederick Charles Morgan,
late Chief Steward of the City of Hereford

THE
LEON VALLEY

Three Herefordshire Villages

INGSLAND, MONKLAND & EARDISLAND

by

NORMAN C. REEVES

PHILLIMORE

1980

Published by
PHILLIMORE & CO. LTD.
London and Chichester

Head Office: Shopwyke Hall,
Chichester, Sussex, England

ISBN 0 85033 347 4

Printed in Great Britain by
UNWIN BROTHERS LTD.
at the Gresham Press, Old Woking, Surrey

and bound at
THE NEWDIGATE PRESS
Book House, Dorking, Surrey

CONTENTS

LIST OF PLATES

EARDISLAND

(between pages 116 and 117)

LIST OF DRAWINGS

FOREWORD

A year or so ago I completed a history of the village of Monkland which had been requested by the vicar, the Rev. John Clingo. Monkland is one of the three villages whose names share the termination 'land', a corruption of the word 'lene', the name of the area drained by and bounded north and south by the rivers Lugg and Arrow. The history of Monkland proved so interesting that I decided to extend my researches to the other two villages, Kingsland and Eardisland.

I had been acquainted with Kingsland since 1947 when, with a fellow schoolmaster, I accompanied a party of boys from the Smethwick Grammar School to a Harvest Camp whose headquarters was St. Mary's Farm. The warm welcome extended to us by Mr. Cecil Price and his wife Dora endeared the place to us, and when, after my retirement, I came to live in Leominster, I renewed my acquaintance with the Prices and their delightful village.

In 1947 I never suspected that I should one day come to know the village and its inhabitants as intimately as I do now, but the extraction of the village's history from documents, newspapers and books, as well as from living people's memories has proved absorbing to me. I now present the results of my researches so that others may share my pleasure.

ACKNOWLEDGEMENTS

For encouragement and help in my research into Kingsland's history I must specially thank the following:

First and foremost, Mrs. Dora Price, my oldest Herefordshire friend; the Rev. Prebendary H. S. G. Thomas, former rector, who has freely allowed me to make use of the invaluable church registers, and assisted in many ways; Mr. F. C. Morgan and his daughter, Miss Penelope Morgan, the librarians of the Cathedral Library, always generous with their help and advice; the staff of the County Council Record Office, especially Miss Jancey and Miss Susan Hubbard; Mr. R. J. Hill of the Hereford City Library; a number of Kingsland people have been most helpful, Mrs. A. G. Shepherd, Mrs. Miles and her daughter, Mrs. Sankey, Captain Hamlen-Williams, Mr. E. Passey, Mrs. E. I. Goodman, and Mr. Heber Langford. Mrs. Jack Cooper has been good enough to draw my attention to documents in her husband's possession relating to Kingsland. Mr. W. D. Turton, solicitor of Leominster, has readily allowed me access to his interesting collection of old maps.

Chapter One

EARLY HISTORY

THE VILLAGE of Kingsland is one of three in north-west Herefordshire whose names terminate with the element 'land'. The others, its near neighbours, are Eardisland and Monkland. The final element of their names was earlier spelt 'lone', 'lane', or 'lene'. The element *lene* or *leon* is contained in a modified form in the names of Leominster (Leon-minster) and Lyonshall (Leon hals), both in the same region. And near Pembridge there is a farm called 'the Leen'.[1] Domesday book even names a Leen hundred. The leen appears to have been the name of the area or plain drained by the rivers Lugg and Arrow, and the word probably refers to the flowing waters of these streams. Leen is the name of a river in Nottinghamshire. The etymologists postulate the root 'lei'—to flow—represented in Welsh by 'lliant' —stream.

When the Mercian prince Merewalh occupied this region, *c.* 600 A.D., he endowed with much land the monastic community he founded at Leominster, but reserved a part of the Lene for his own use. This came to be called 'Kingslene', our modern Kingsland.[2] He is said to have built a castle or fortified place there, and the motte and bailey west of the church are said to be the remaining signs of its position, although they (like so many in this Welsh borderland) could be Norman. Eardisland has two such mottes.

The parish of Kingsland occupies a fertile area between the rivers Lugg and Pinsley, the latter being a minor stream which takes its origin in Shobdon Marsh. The parish is more or less bounded on the west by the great Roman road which ran northwards from Caerleon to Chester, forming a means of

1

Plan of Motte and Bailey, Kingsland

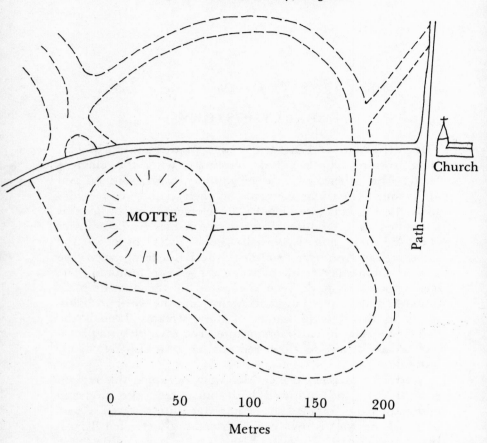

communication between the two legionary fortresses. On it lay Street, once a separate manor with its own chapel, but now represented by Street Court. Street probably existed before Kingsland, for we have no reason to believe that Kingsland existed before Merewalh's time. The site of the village may have been chosen for reasons of defence, for it was protected by rivers to the north and south, and by Cursneh Hill to the east. The rivers also ensured a plentiful water supply which was lacking in Street, thus inhibiting its growth.

The area surrounding this residence defended by moats was very fertile and hence valuable. Kenelm, a Mercian prince who flourished just before the Norman Conquest, expressly excluded Kingsland from his pious or charitable bequests. An inscription formerly in Leominster church bore the following words:

> My father did build upon this my town
> I have loved Christ and for his love my lands I forsook,
> But my Kingsland and my Kenelmworth I do not forsake
> I am Christ's Kenelm and Kenelmbald is my kinsman.

(This is only an extract from a fairly lengthy inscription on a brass plate in Leominster church copied by Hackluyt in 1592.)

Nothing certain is known of Kingland's history between its foundation by Merewalh and the Norman Conquest. It had a church and clergy, but their names are unknown.

After the Norman Conquest Herefordshire was entrusted to William Fitz Osbern, who remained Earl of Hereford until his death in 1071. He gave the churches (i.e., the tithes of the churches) of Lene (Kingsland) and Marden to the abbey he had founded in the place of his birth in Normandy, Cormeilles. The successor to the earldom joined in a revolt against King William in 1075; the revolt was put down and the leaders lost their lands. The earldom of Herefordshire was abolished and was not revived until the reign of Stephen. Kingsland and Marden reverted to the Crown.

Kingsland features in the Balliol 'Herefordshire Domesday' manuscript, thought to have been composed between 1160 and 1170: 'The King holds lene [a note explains this as 'kingsleane'] which King Edward held formerly'.

This 'lene' is said to consist of 15 hides (a hide being approximately 120 acres), with five ploughs, and there could be three more, 21 villeins, nine bordars, with 17 more ploughs, 10 oxmen, two serfs, six 'coliberti' or freed serfs, and two mills. Kingsland was evidently a large and important manor.

The Domesday Book of 1086 says that 'of this manor' Ralph de Mortimer holds one 'membrum', i.e., an outlying estate;[3] and Roger de Laci one manor of two hides called Hope, another of one hide called Lestret (Street) and another of one hide called Lautone (Lawton).

Another 'lene' described in Domesday Book as belonging to the king and as formerly the property of Earl Morcar must be Eardisland, the 'Earl's lene'. This, too, covered 15 hides. The *Victoria County History* for Herefordshire remarks that the two manors 'seem to have descended together through Braose to Mortimer,[4] and there is evidence that the Braoses had a chief seat at Kingsland, from which doubtless William De Braose [in 1210] made his furious raid on Leominster, when he burst into revolt in the reign of John'.

Of the Manor of Street Domesday Book remarks that it is in the hands of Roger de Laci and that King Edward formerly had it.

S. R. Meyrick, the historian and antiquarian, writing in 1826 in the *Gentleman's Magazine,* says:'About 300 yards from the House of Street was formerly a chapel,[5] long since destroyed, but a brass plate with a black letter inscription from one of the monuments there has been preserved . . .'.

'Here lyeth Anne the wyfe of Edward Hall, ye daughter of Sr Percifal Harte K^{nt}, her mother, daughter and one of the co-heires of the Lord Braye, which Anne deceased the 29th of September A.D. 1594'.

In the quatrefoil of the window in the north wall of the organ chamber[6] of Kingsland church is a piece of glass which is said to have come from this Street chapel, and which bears the arms of Auffrick, Isle of Man.

NOTES

1. O.S. 383 592.
2. The final 'd' used not to be pronounced by natives.
3. Mereston, the modern Marston.
4. The families were related by marriage. Eleanor, daughter of William de Braose, and wife of Humphrey de Bohun (VI), received the Lordship of Brecon together with Huntington, Eardisland and Kingsland (1254). Cal. Patent Rolls, 1252, 1254.
5. The bishops' registers contain no references to appointments of clergy to this chapel, so it must have been served from a neighbouring church. The only reference to it which I have found is in the register of Bishop Edmund Lacy under the date 1419: *Idem prior (de Leominstria) possidet porcionem in capellis de Strete et Crofte taxatam ad ii s.*

Chapter Two

THE CHURCH

WITH THE POSSIBLE EXCEPTION of the motte and its surrounding earthworks, the oldest existing building in Kingsland is the church. This was begun *c.* 1290 A.D., with the help, no doubt considerable, of Edmund Mortimer, the seventh Lord of Wigmore. It replaced an earlier church of which two, almost invisible, small lancet windows (which must have been the east windows of the aisles) may be the only surviving evidence.

The stone for the building of the church is said to have been quarried on the Tarrs, the hill about two km. NNW. of the church (O.S. 442 632). If this is so, it was probably conveyed at least part of the way by water. On the ridge of the Tarrs there once stood an upright monolith, called 'The Warrior's Grave'. 'Near it', wrote Jobling, 'there used to be a bastion about 30 yards long, with side wings projecting from it for about the same distance.' Its date and purpose are at any rate unknown.

Jobling also reported that in the shingle under the Tarrs 'a Saxon stone mortar for grinding corn' was found, and was later placed in Hereford museum. It is surprising, considering its Saxon foundation, that no other Saxon finds have been reported from Kingsland. .

The size of the church, for it was not a monastic foundation, witnesses to the considerable population of Kingsland in the 13th century. From that period, at least, it was a well endowed rectory, and its rectors were often men of considerable importance in the diocese.

As Pevsner remarks, the building is 'all of a piece', being almost as it left the hands of the builders in the early 14th century. The little Volka chapel, opening eastwards from the north porch, and the south porch, were added in the 15th century. The church consists of a chancel with a nave flanked by north and south aisles and a fine western tower.

The curious Volka chapel is clearly a chantry chapel. Along the wall on the right of the altar lies a lidless, empty stone coffin. The name of this unusually-sited chapel has given rise to much speculation in the past. One theory was that it was the burial place of the church's founder, Edmund Mortimer, but he was, in fact, buried at Wigmore Abbey. Another was that it once housed a holy hermit who spent his nights in the empty coffin to remind him of his last end. The name Volka or Vaukel has not been found in documents earlier than the late 17th century. The most likely explanation is that it is a memorial chapel to an early benefactor of the church, who was once the occupant of the stone coffin. Possibly, because of Reformation fears of its superstitious use, its contents were destroyed and it was left lidless. R. H. George, writing in the Woolhope Club's transactions for 1915, suggests another possibility: that the chapel was the burial place of Walter de Mortimer, the rector of 1315. Walter, or 'Gaultier' in Norman French, could have been corrupted to Volka.

There was certainly a chantry chapel in Kingsland church, that of Our Lady. The two stipendiaries of this altar were well endowed with tenements and lands.[1] Besides celebrating the mass, the chantry priest acted as a schoolmaster to the children of the parish. In the survey of Edward VI, 1547, the one remaining chantry priest, Sir John Harteley, is described as 'of good conversation, aged 42, who celebrates, helps the curate [i.e., the vicar], keepeth a school and doth bring up youth virtuously . . . and hath the clear revenue and profit of his scholars. Net value £8.4.3'.

The masses for the dead continued to be offered undisguised up to the reign of Elizabeth.

In a document dated 27 May 1557, the lands belonging to one of the chantries are named: 'Whereas by patent under the great seal of the Court of Augmentation, 23 Feb. 3 Ed. VI., were leased for 21 years to John Wall gent. *inter*

Kingsland Church, Hereford, N.E. 1826

alia all lands known as "Hilles House", "le Scholehouse", "Sednolles", "Sir Thomas Close" and "Lamesyche" in Kyngesland in Stratforde hundred, co. Hereford formerly belonging to the chantry called "Kyngeslande" there, except great trees and woods, at a yearly rent, for these and other lands contained in the said patent, of 91*l*. 2s. 9d.'.

A document at the Public Record Office,[2] of which the Cathedral Library at Hereford has a transcript, records the dedication of a chantry in Kingsland church which was founded by King Edward IV. The king is said to have endowed the service of 'St. Katyne of Charitie to praye for the soulles of all those that were slayne in battal at Mortym's Cross'. It is not unreasonable to suppose, as others have done, that this chantry was the Volka Chapel. After all 'Volka' suggests folk, perhaps referring to the multitude of the battle's victims. One of Leominster's commons was called the Volka and here it clearly implies 'land belonging to the folk'. Perhaps the coffin in the chapel was that of an important leader, or of an 'unknown soldier' representing the nameless dead.

The most surprising thing about Kingsland church is the survival of the stained glass of its east window. This dates from the 14th century and is thus almost coeval with the fabric. It bears the arms of Dame Matilda Mortimer,[3] the lady who presented the first known rector in 1285. In the topmost light of the tracery, Christ is shown holding a cross and seated on a rainbow. Below this in two lights is the Coronation of the Blessed Virgin. The main panels of the window represent the four great archangels, a grouping which is said to be unique: Michael, to whom the church is dedicated, spearing a red and snake-like dragon; Raphael, accompanied by Tobias with the miraculous fish; Gabriel making his stupendous announcement to Mary; and Uriel with the prophet Esdras, who bears a scroll with his name. The window is rich in red, blue and gold colouring.

The church was thoroughly restored by the architect G. F. Bodley, in 1867, care being taken not to destroy any of its ancient features. The nave and aisles were fitted with oak benches and the chancel with oak stalls. The chancel was paved with Godwin's tiles and its ceiling was painted as we now see it. The roof of the nave, previously ceiled, was opened out and restored.

NOTES

1. See extract from Chantry Certificate appended to this chapter.
2. P.R.O. E.301, Nos. 24, 25, 26.
3. E.C.H.M. says the shield bears the arms of de Braose of Brecon, but the Mortimers were descended from them (see p. 4).

APPENDIX TO CHAPTER TWO

Extract from Chantry Certificate for Herefordshire (P.R.O. E.301/34) for 1548

(Folio 62v)

No. 110. *Lands of Servesse in the Paryshe of Kingesland*

In the tenure of Thomas Colman a tenement in Over Lawton	23s 4d
Of William ap Gwilym for a parcel of meadow ground ..	5s 4d
Of Rychard Colman for a rent from his freehold	13d

Of Thomas Colman for a tenement called Beddowes   ..   29s 4d
Of John Taylor for one acre of meadow in Brodmedowe ..   12d
Of Thomas Pyvynch for two acres of meadow in Brodmedowe   3s
Of John A Knyll for a messuage with appurtenances called Rodes
    ground 20s
Of Walter Mascall for a parcel of meadow called Wylman Shyre   12s
Of Harry Roweall for a tenement and three acres of land called
    Inchemarshe 7s
Of Thomas Pyvynche for a parcel of pasture..   ..   ..   18d
Of Thomas Henound of Marton for land 22s 8d
Of Humfrey More nowe deceased for a meadow plocke in
    Lyddicotte 5d
Of Thomas Colman for a cottage called Sir Thomas Cottage   3s
Of Thomas Taylor and John Colman for one pasture called
    Lane Syche 11s
Of John Kyngton for one parcel of meadow which rent is for
    drawyn for the space of eight years 2s 8d

(Folio 63r)
Of John a Knyll gent for a parcel of meadow lying in Brodmedowe
    the rent hath been withdrawen these six years and more   22d
Of Thomas Pyvynch for one pasture called Hockblock the rent
    hath been withdrawen three years or thereabouts   ..   2s 8d
Of Thomas Pyvynch, bocher, for a parcel of meadow lying in
    Brodmedowe rent hath been withdrawen ten years and above   8d

Customary Tenaunts

William Wall for a cottage called Coter off the Quenes custom-
    hold in the custom, rent dew to the Quene 6s
One garden by John Whetston's house 6d
Our Ladye Meadow 17s 6d
Ten acres of errable land 5s
A burgage in the tenure of Hewe ap Resse 2s 8d
One acres of pasture in Lyttle Sarnesfeld 2d
Tanne House 2s
One burgage 6d
                                                                  ———
                                                 Sum   ..   54s 1d

Rents Resolute

To the Lord Ferress 17s 6d
To Mr Monyngton 4d
To the Lord Ferress 1½d
                                                                  ———
                                              Sum reprises ..   17s 11½d
                                              And remains clear   ..   36s 1½d

(Folio 62[b])

After my hartie comendacions, whereas John Wall one of the Kings Majesties Buttery hath in lease of the Kings Majesties gyfte under the scale of this court the chantrys of Kingesland and Dylwyn in the Countie of Hereford letting you to understande that the same John Wall hath a grante made unto him for the purchasing therefore wherefore these we require you furthwith upon the first here to make a note in your bokes that the said John Wall hath a graunt thereof and that you do not make or deliver any particulars herein to any person or persons but only the said John Wall the bringer hereof although I or any other should unadvysedly signe any warrant for the particulars of the same whereby the said John Wall might be prevented or hyndered in his suite This fare you well from . . . in London the 12 of June 1552 your loving frend Ryc Sakevyle.

Of Walter Loggar & Ales Freman for acres of errable land and pasture costomhold	9s
One house poynted for a scolle house parcel of the Quenes custome ground	6s
Of Thomas Strvyn for a cotage of the customhold called Hyalles house	8s
Of Rychard Deswall for a tenement with appurtenances and land called Sedmolles	11s 4d
Of John Kyngton for a pasture called Howlward rent hath withdrawn five years and more	6s 8d
Of John Umble for 3 acres of errable land rent hath been withdrawn 9 years and more	6d
Sum	£9 (6s 8d) 16d

Rents Resolute

Paid to the Quenes Grace	12d
Paid to the heyres of John Monyngton	10d
Paid to the Quenes Grace	12d
Paid to the heirs of Mr Monyngton	10d
Paid to Wyllyam Berryngton	2s
Paid to William Gryseman	6d
Paid to the Quenes Grace	2s
Paid to John Juke	9s
Paid to the Quenes Grace for custom rent	2s
Paid to the Quenes Grace for custom rent	2s

(Folio 63v)

Paid to the Quenes Grace for custom rent	2s
Paid to her Grace for custom rent	2s
Paid to her Grace for custom rent	4s
Paid to John Blunt gent for cheffe rent	7d
To the Quenes Grace for cheffe rent	2s
Sum reprises	31s. 9d
And so remains clear	£8 4s. 4d

No. 111 *Lampes in the Parishe of Kynglands*

One acre of land in the tenure of John Trumper to maintain a lampe	2d

No. 118. *Ereslande*

Two gallons of Oyle from the land of the Trynyte in the
    paryshe of Leominster 2s

One acre of land in Estefeld at Eresland to maintain a lampe
    in the tenure of Raffe Dyggar 4d

                                                            2s 4d

No. 119. *Monkland:* Lands in the tenure of Walter Seward to
    maintain a lyght 5s 2d

Chapter Three

THE BATTLE OF MORTIMER'S CROSS

THE SPECULATION about the origin of the Volka chapel reminds one that the most important event which involved Kingsland was the battle which led to the coronation of a Mortimer as king of England.

The misgovernment of the country under the pious but inept Henry VI led to widespread discontent and gave Richard, Duke of York, an opportunity to assert his right to the throne. He could claim to be the legitimate king as a direct descendant of Edward III, and through his mother, Ann Mortimer. His faction, promising firm government, was favoured by the powerful merchants of London and the manufacturers of Kent. Henry VI's Lancastrian party received its strongest support from the wild Welsh and the even wilder people of the north and west. Henry himself was not militant, but his vigorous wife, Margaret, fought like a tigress for her husband and her little son. Her army was victorious over the Yorkists at Wakefield. Richard was captured and ignominiously beheaded at York. His 17-year-old son, Edward, was at the time marching north with an army composed largely of his Herefordshire tenants when he learned both of his father's defeat and of a projected attack upon his castles of Wigmore and Ludlow. He therefore wheeled westwards to Shrewsbury and marched south through Ludlow, Richard's Castle, Bircher and Lucton towards Kingsland, to block the enemy's advance up the valley through Aymestrey to Wigmore, which was held by his mother.

The Lancastrian army had already occupied Leominster and Cursneh Hill, from which they had dislodged Edward's

13

loyal supporters. The army supporting Queen Margaret
and Henry consisted mainly of Welsh and Irish kerns who
were led by the Earl of Ormonde, the Earl of Pembroke
and Owen Tudor. The two armies faced one another in
the plain of Kingsland between the rivers Lugg and Pinsley
on Candlemas Day 1461.

To avoid the loss of many innocent lives Edward, Earl of
March, offered through his herald Bluemantle to settle the
dispute by fighting the Earl of Pembroke in single combat.
The Bluemantle Cottages[1] are said to mark the spot where
this challenge was refused, so the opposing sides prepared
for the struggle. Snow lay on the ground, but the sky was
clear; some optical illusion made the sun appear as three.
The quick-witted Edward interpreted this as an omen in his
favour. One writer declares that his words were: 'Yonder 3
suns are the 3 Lancastrian leaders, Pembroke, Tudor and
Wiltshire [Earl of Ormonde] whose glory shall this day
centre on me!'

A 15th-century chronicle has another story which, it
seems to me, might have had more effect on those God-
fearing peasants. 'The noble Earl Edward them comforted
and said, "Be-eth of good comfort and dreadeth not; this
is a good sign, for these three suns betoken the Father, the
Son and the Holy Ghost, and therefore let us have a good
heart, and in the name of Almighty God go we against
our enemies". Then the Earl kneeled down and made his
prayers and thanked God.'[2]

The Great West Field of Kingsland then became a scene
of carnage. The Lancastrian force under Pembroke broke
through Edward's line and pursued his supporters up the
valley through Aymestrey nearly as far as Wigmore, but
when the exultant troops returned they found that
Edward's centre and left had prevailed. They also learnt
that the Yorkist supporters in Leominster had risen and
asserted themselves by seizing the unguarded baggage of
the enemy at Kingsland. Though the Lancastrians fought on
desperately, by the end of the day they were utterly defeated;
It is said (by Halle) that 3,800 of them fell in the battle.
Of their opponents the numbers of dead are given as four

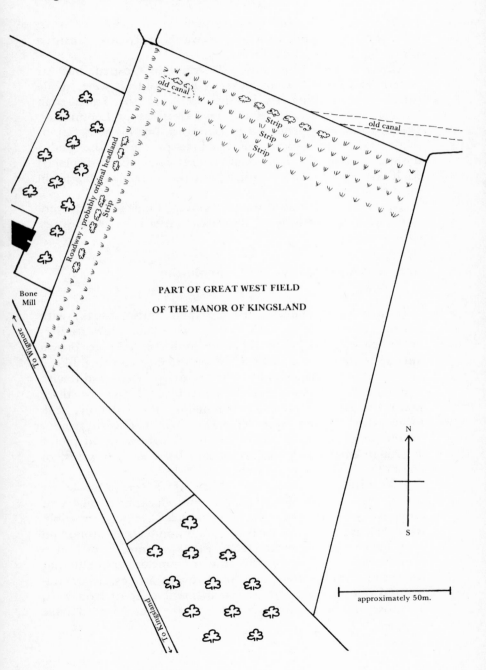

old canal

old canal

Strip
Strip
Strip

Roadway - probably original headland

Strip

Bone
Mill

To Wigmore

PART OF GREAT WEST FIELD
OF THE MANOR OF KINGSLAND

To Kingsland

N

S

approximately 50m.

to five hundred. Edward's victory at Mortimer's Cross, followed by another shortly afterwards at Towton, ensured his coronation as Edward IV.

The Earls of Pembroke and Ormonde escaped, but Sir Owen Tudor and four other Welsh leaders were made prisoner. According to Blount, some of the Lancastrian leaders were executed at the Five Crosses[3] at Leominster. Owen Tudor was beheaded in Hereford, but his son, Jasper, made good his escape and lived to procreate the Tudor dynasty which in less than twenty-five years displaced Richard III, Edward's brother, and put a Lancastrian again on the throne.

The dead were buried in mass graves, some of which were noticed by gravediggers in recent times in Aymestrey churchyard.

Arms and Armour at the Battle of Mortimer's Cross

In this battle the knights and their squires fought with sword, lance, mace and battle-axe. The foot soldiers depended entirely upon the pike and the popular 'brown bill'. The latter was a horrible weapon, something like a modern hedge-slasher, but with a sharp point, and with double razor edges from which projected two or three sharp spikes. The archers used mainly the longbow, and, though the knights were replacing chain-mail with armour of tempered steel, an arrow from a longbow could pierce a mailed knight through breast and back at 250 yards, or nail both his thighs to his horse at one shot.

It is often wondered why relics of the great battle are not found in abundance on the site. Occasional pieces of arms and armour have been found which have been (possibly wrongly) ascribed to this period. Cannon-balls of stone and iron have been reported from time to time, but though cannon were in use at the time it appears unlikely that they were transported by these roving armies, who confronted one another almost unexpectedly. Apart from this, in those days of universal poverty, the dead would have been stripped of any arms or armour of value immediately after the battle.

In 1799 an inscribed tablet was erected at the junction of the A.4110 and B.4360 roads NW. of Kingsland (O.S. 436 619) to commemorate the battle and mark its site. This had become eroded by 1974 and was then replaced by another, as far as possible identical to it. The public house at this junction is named *The Monument.*

FOOTNOTES

1. O.S. 426 632.
2. Davies' *English Chronicle*, 110. *Three Fifteenth Century Chronicles*, 77.
3. Now called the Iron Cross.

Chapter Four

THE MANOR

AS WE SEE in Chapter One, until it was granted to the Braoses or the Mortimers Kingsland was a royal manor. When, after the battles of Mortimer's Cross and Towton, Edward Plantagenet ascended the throne as Edward IV, it again became royal property. In the reign of Charles I it was the property of Queen Henrietta Maria. Later, it formed the jointure of Catherine of Braganza, the dowager of King Charles II. Shortly after this it was sold to Lord Coningsby, whose descendant, Viscount Malden, sold it to the Rev. Richard Evans in 1793. It remained in his family until the death of Richard Davies Evans when it passed in 1871 to the Right Honourable Lord Bateman, second Baron Bateman. In 1900 George Denison Faber, afterwards Baron Wittenham, acquired it. The manor was acquired in 1919 by Captain the Honourable Charles Stanhope Melville Bateman Hanbury. In 1922 it passed through the hands of Wm. George Prior, Esq., of Leominster, the estate agent of Lord Bateman, and Sir John Wood, Baronet. In this same year (1922) the Real Property Act swept away all manors.

The court of the manor or court leet regulated the life of the village, and this was held annually, the bailiff of the court being present with the suit roll. At the court of April 1733 there were 84 tenants present, 56 were 'essoined' or excused, and 12 defaulted. Up to the year before, the rolls were kept in Latin, and the steward occasionally had difficulty in Latinising certain English words: *postis flagellandi* rendered whipping-post, but *taurus variegatus* was the best he could do to render 'brindled' bull.

18

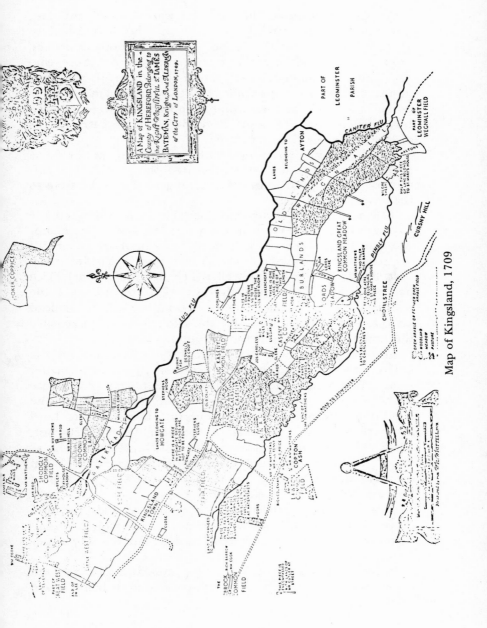

Map of Kingsland, 1709

At these meetings the tenants who formed the jury 'presented' or brought forward those who had failed to observe the rules for the proper maintenance of the hedges, ditches, gates and water-courses on the manor; those who had put more animals than allowed for them on the commons, and those responsible for the maintenance of the pound, the stocks and the whipping-post. Fines were imposed for absence from the court, and for failure to carry out its orders within the time stipulated.

Apart from 'presenting' those guilty of minor local irregularities, the jury also presented the death of a customary tenant and the court arranged the succession to the property.

This transfer of ownership, or 'alienation', involved the payment of a fine by the new tenant. The lord of the manor was also entitled to claim a 'heriot' on the death of one of his tenants. In Kingsland this heriot was 'a Yoake of the best Beasts or the best Jewell which he (the tenant) dieth possessed of'. The Court Roll of 1716 records that the bailiff had seized one black and one brindled bull for the lord on the death of a tenant. By the end of the 18th century this had been compounded for a sum of 10 guineas.

In some cases, where the property was small and the tenants poor, the lord had been content to accept a smaller sum. Thomas Sale, the steward of the manor in 1858 wrote to a prospective buyer of the manor telling him of the conditions prevailing in the property. He said: 'The Lord has received few heriots since the year 1846—£270—but, being the resident Rector of the Parish, Richard Davies Evans has never enforced his just rights. As far as I can ascertain the number of heriots payable is 118. My fees as Steward average £20 a year clear'.

A widow was entitled to the whole of the copyhold property for her life as her freebench or dower. She paid a fine of 1d. on her admission and a rent of 8s. 8d. per annum.

In former times the payment of a heriot was also expected on alienation, but there is no evidence of such being seized after 1744.

1. Motte and bailey, Kingsland, said to be the remaining signs of the position of a castle or fortified place built by the Mercian prince Merewalh.

2. Kingsland Church. This building was begun about 1290, replacing an earlier church.

4. The Volka chapel, Kingsland church.

3. Interior view of Kingsland church.

The jury of the court imposed fines varying between 2d. and £1 19s. 10d. It also appointed the petty constables of the townships of West Town, Longford, Aston and Lawton.

The last Court Leet and View of Free Pledge was held at Kingsland in 1854, and the Real Property Act of 1922 finally abolished all manorial courts.

Open-field cultivation had been practised in Kingsland until the late 18th century. A map of 1709 shows a number of large open fields: Great West Field, Little West Field, and Bore Field. Others are Kindon Common Field, Lug Caseny Common Field, Kingsland Great Common Meadow, Caseny Common Field and Fair Field. The last, which was just south of the church, was the site of the annual fair.

The Act for the Enclosure of the Open and Common Fields in the townships of Upper and Lower Lawton, West Town, Longford and Aston received the royal assent on 17 June 1814, and thereafter 140 acres of heaths, commons and wastes were enclosed.

Before the official enclosures authorised in the Act of 1814 areas of waste land had from time to time been enclosed as small holdings, and recognised by the manorial court. The lord of the manor then exacted a rent from those who made the encroachment on his property.

The Hampton Court Estate terriers of 1780 list some of these 'New Encroachments on the manor of Kingsland:

'John Wharton, a new erected Cottage and about 20 perches of Garden at Aston. Yearly value £1. Jeremiah Beavan, a Cottage and about 20 perches of Garden. Yearly value 25s.

'George Davies, a miserable Hovel and about 30 perches of Garden at Shirley heath. Yearly value 10s.

'W. Bayliss, a new erected Cottage and about 20 perches of Garden in Lug Lane. Yearly value of 25s.

'John Hughes, a Cottage and about 10 perches of Garden in Howfoort [Hereford] Lane. Yearly value 15s.

'John Bowen, a Cottage and about 8 perches of Garden at Bucknell. Yearly value £1.

'Samuel Wanklin, a very ordinary Cottage and about 10 perches of Garden at Bucknell. Yearly value 10s.'.

A later Act of 1829 authorised further enclosure of common fields, commons and heaths in the parishes of Aymestrey and Kingsland; this enclosure included commonable lands in Upper and Lower Lawton, West Town, Longford and Aston in the parish of Kingsland. The effect of this enclosure may be seen by comparing the map of 1709 with a modern map of Kingsland, where one finds a small number of consolidated farms, each with its own farmhouse.

Much ground was saved by the abolition of the many strips cultivated by individual tenants in the open fields, because they were separated by uncultivated baulks (called 'meres' locally), which disappeared on enclosure. The lord was the owner of minerals and woods, so the tenants were not enthusiastic about growing or planting trees.

Chapter Five

ECCLESIASTICAL HISTORY

Rectors

THOUGH THERE was a church in Kingsland in Saxon and early Norman times, we have no records of its clergy before 1285. Since that date, owing to the survival of the bishops' registers from that of Thomas de Cantilupe onwards, we have a complete list of the rectors.

These men were often important clergy, sometimes canons of the Cathedral. Being in general senior clergy they were required by the bishop to regulate the affairs of other clergy. For instance, on 12 December 1385, Roger Nash, rector of Kingsland, was empowered to enquire into the alleged immorality of William the parson of Monkland and to award due punishment.

Just as the late 13th-century church owed its existence to the powerful Mortimer family, it is not surprising to find that the family acted as the patrons of the living over a long period. In the list which follows, the name of the patron is given when this is known. In a few cases the date of the rector's institution is now known; his name is mentioned in the bishop's register when his successor was instituted. Thus Richard Talbot was appointed in 1410 'on the death of John Catesby'.

There were occasional disputes over the patronage. In 1460 Bishop John Stanbury has the entry: 'Whereas the Duke of York has presented Thomas Walford to the church of Kingsland, and a certain Thomas Downe claims to be already rector, the bishop commissions Richard Pede to examine the title of the latter, and if he fails to make it good, to institute Walford'.

Date of Institution	Rector presented	Cause of change	Patron(s)
1285	Geoffrey de Balecote		Dame Matilda Mortimer
1304	William Mortimer		Dame Margaret Mortimer
1315	Walter de Mortimer		
1328	William de Ford		Lady Margaret Mortimer
1342	William de Retford	resigned	the Crown
1350	John de Shipedham		Sir Roger de Mortimer
1353	William de Pembrugge		
	William Davy or David	died	
1384	John Piers	exchanged	Peter de la Mare
	Roger Nasshe	died	Hugh Cheyne
1388	William de Ford		the Bishop, etc.
	John Catesby		
1410	Richard Talbot	exchanged	the King
1412	John Ingayne, or Lyngeyne		
1415	William Batysford	exchanged	Edmund, Earl of March
1428	Thomas Ledsam		
1429	Henry Hanslape		the Crown
	John Bosham	died	
1444	Walter Johan	died	Richard, duke of York
1460	Thomas Downe	died	the King
1489	William Grave		Cecily, Duchess of York
	John Rede	died	
1521	Peter Roderick	died	Queen Katherine
1524	Thomas Payne, M.A.	resigned	
1548	Edmund Danyell, M.A.	deposed, deprived	John Chambers and George Owen, M.D.*
1559	Thomas Taylor		
1579	Griffin Lewis, S.T.D.	no cause given	Henry Vernon and Anne Talbot, his wife, d. of John, earl of Shrewsbury
1607	Sylvanus Griffiths, D.D.		the King
1624	John Hughes, D.D	died 1648	
1648	Tim Woodroffe	died 1678	Sir Robert Harley
1678	John Slade, M.A.	died	two persons: Littleton Powis, Thomas Powis
1720	John Davies, D.D.	died	two persons
1733	Hugh Morgan	resigned	two persons
1734	Sneyd Davies, B.A.	died	two persons
1769	Richard Evans, M.A.	cession	himself
1794	Richard Evans, M.A.	died	himself
1797	Richard David Evans, B.A.	died	
1821	William Evans	resigned	
1841	Richard Davies Evans, B.A.	died	two persons
1871	William Goss	resigned	
1876	William Henry Bradley, M.A.		

*By grant from late King Henry VIII.

Date of Institution	Rector presented	Cause of change	Patron(s)
1884	Thomas George Hamilton-Baillie		
1917	James Jobling		Mrs. Hamlen Williams
1925	George Henzell Jobling		
1954	Godfrey Worsley		
1961	Michael Wilson		
1965	Herbert S. G. Thomas		
1976	J. G. Williams		

Notes on Some Rectors

William Davy or David, died as rector of Kingsland on 16 October 1383; he appears to have been ordained as priest in 1348. At the time of his death he occupied a canonical residence in the Close at Hereford.

John Catesby was present at the election of the Dean in 1393. He vacated Colwall on 25 September 1390 and was collated to a canonical house in 1398.

In 1384 the bishop's register records some dispute over the patronage of Kingsland rectory. 'It belonged to the late Earl of March. The king permitted him to grant it to his executors, and that Hugh Cheyne and Peter de la Mare, and not the Earl of Northumberland, are his executors.'

Edmund Daniel, appointed rector in 1548, was a graduate and Fellow of Merton College, Oxford. He was Dean of Hereford in 1559 when, shortly after Elizabeth's accession, he was tendered the oaths of supremacy and allegiance; he refused to take the oaths and so was deprived of both offices. He was committed to the custody of the Marquis of Winchester, but escaped to the Continent, and he was in Rome by 1564. He died there in 1576, and was buried in the chapel of the English College. From the following note it would appear that the Reformation did not affect Kingsland before Daniel's departure: 'In Kingsland is a chauntry for our ladyes Service in which were divers praists services wch continued undisguised till the reign of Queen Elizabeth'.

Thomas Taylor, who replaced Daniel at Kingsland, was instituted to the vicarage of Bromyard in 1564—presumably he held both livings. In 1542 he had been presented by Henry VIII to the vicarage of Byton, and in 1550 he was appointed to Shobdon. Like the 'vicar of Bray', he was obviously very compliant, obliging Henry VIII, Edward VI, Mary and Elizabeth—a fitting successor to Edmund Daniel!

Sylvanus Griffiths, D.D. This rector was born in Herefordshire. In 1590 he matriculated, aged 14, at Brasenose College, Oxford and· became Doctor of Divinity in 1610. By 1604 he was Treasurer of Hereford Cathedral and a canon. In the same year he was made rector of Hampton Bishop. He was Archdeacon of Hereford in 1606, rector of Kingsland in 1607, and of Hopesay, Shropshire, in 1609. In 1617 he was created Dean of Hereford.

John Hughes, D.D. succeeded Sylvanus Griffiths in 1624 when the famous Francis Godwin was Bishop of Hereford; Hughes was, in fact, the bishop's son-in-law. In his *Man in the Moone,* which relates the adventures of a Spaniard who caused himself to be transported to the moon by an eagle-like bird, Francis Godwin anticipated by centuries similar fantasies by Jules Verne and H. G. Wells. This was clearly a contrast to his usual writing which consisted of learned histories in Latin. Godwin's nepotism began before he was appointed to Hereford, for as Bishop of Llandaff he enriched his own family by preferment in the diocese. Elizabeth, who was queen at this time, was annoyed at this misuse of the revenues of the see, and expressed a dislike of bishops marrying for this very reason.

It would appear that Dr. Hughes shared the widespread belief in astrology which marked the early 17th century, for when he baptised his son in 1627 he made the following unusual entry in the register: 'Charles the sonne of John Hughes D.D. baptised IX December and borne the XXVI daie of November about one of the clock after midnight'. He had not been so precise when he baptised his daughter Susanna in 1624.

In their report of 6 July 1641, the Commissioners of Charitable Uses accused Dr. Hughes of retaining for his own use much of the endowment bequeathed in 1607 by William Whittington of Street for the maintenance of a school and schoolmaster in Eardisland. For 17 years, they said, he had deprived the school of £4 per annum. Furthermore, he had received £15 for wool sold in Street, £10 of which rightly belonged to the Eardisland schoolmaster. Hughes was ordered to pay £78 before the following September, but there is no evidence that this was done.

One gets the impression that the Puritan Commissioners disliked John Hughes, for in 1642 they reported: 'Dr. Hughes, rector, archdeacon of Hereford and vicar of Newland . . . seldom preacheth and hath preached against preaching, nor procures hee any to do it for him'.

At this time Dr. Hughes had bought the perpetual advowson (right of presentation to the benefice). The possession of this right passed later to the Evans family, members of which were rectors from 1769 to 1871; we thus find the first two presenting themselves to the living.

Dr. Hughes was buried in the chancel of his parish church. On the slab (now in the floor of the tower) which formerly covered his remains was a Latin epitaph which is no longer visible:

> *H. S. E. Joannes Hughes S.T.P. e celebri familia inter Monae Venedoturum Insulares Ortus, Qui cum SS.LL studia potiora sibi potissimum elegisset SS Ordines amplexus, Archidiaconatu Herefordiensi, Praebenda in ecclesia Cathedrali, in Landavensi item altera, Ornatus. Hujus ecclesiae pastorali regimini Praepositus, Eidem complures annos fideliter Praefuit. In motibus Nostratium immotus, Animi, Vitae, Fideique integer, Obiit 7 Idd. Jun. Anno 1648, Fere Septuagenarius. Oliverus Hughes F.N.M. Patri charissimo Parentavit.*

When translated this reads:

Here is buried John Hughes S.T.P. born of a famous family of Anglesey who, after choosing to study with great diligence the Sacred Scriptures, accepted Holy Orders. He obtained the dignity of Archdeacon of Hereford, was rewarded with a prebend in the Cathedral and another in that of Llandaff. He was appointed Rector of this church and performed his duties faithfully over many years. He remained unmoved amid the commotions of our days, unsullied in thought, life and faith. He died 7th June 1648 almost 70 years old. Oliver Hughes, his eldest son, paid this respect to his dearest father.

Timothy Woodroffe was born in 1594, the son of a Wiltshire clergyman. He was educated at Malmesbury under Robert Latymer, who was schoolmaster there for 40 years, and also taught Thomas Hobbes, the famous philosopher. Woodroffe continued his education at Balliol College, Oxford. He attracted the notice of Sir Robert Harley, who invited him to be one of the preachers in the Cathedral of Hereford. In 1649 Harley made him rector of Kingsland, where, in the words of Anthony Wood, 'after many years of painful preaching and much good done in the neighbourhood by the practice of Physick (Wherein he always gave his advice and remedies gratis)', he died. He was buried at Kingsland on 5 August 1678.

As a preacher at the Cathedral, Woodroffe was *persona grata* with the Commonwealth government. In the Bishop's Act Book for 1662 (two years after the Restoration), Kingsland church is reported as having no surplice. As a Puritan Woodroffe no doubt hated any such relic of popery. In that year the schoolmaster, Moses Ludlow, was also presented as unlicensed. Two years later the churchwardens, William Grismond and William Bubb, were presented for failing to provide the church with books of homilies and canons. In 1676 Woodroffe was presented by his own churchwardens for omitting to make the perambulation of the parish in Rogation week, an action which seems rather harsh, as the rector was then eighty-two!

Woodroffe wrote 'A Treatise on Simeon's Song: or Instructions how to live holily and die happily', and dedicated the work to his patron, Sir Robert Harley.

Timothy Woodroffe's son, Benjamin (1638-1711) gained national fame as a scholarly divine. He was successively a chaplain to James, Duke of York, and Charles II. James II nominated him to the Deanery of Christ Church, Oxford, in 1688, but he was not installed. As Principal of Gloucester Hall from 1692 he began its rebuilding. In 1697 he initiated the erection of 'Greek College', the object of which was to promote the union of the Greek Orthodox Church with the Church of England.

John Davies, D.D. (d. 1732), His epitaph describes him as follows: 'Precentor of St. Davids and Prebendary of Hereford and St. Asaph, but much better distinguished by his personal worth than he could have been by the highest station in the church whose doctrines he constantly preached and practised in a manner equalled by few, excelled by no one. Nor was he less remarkable for his public spirit and an unalterable attachment to the interest of his country which engaged him to many and recommended him to all good men'.

Dr. John Davies died at Bath on 14 October 1732. His body was brought to Kingsland and buried on 21 December.

Sneyd Davies, D.D., 1709-1769. Dr. John Davies married Honora, the widow of William Ravenscroft, who had died in 1698. Honora's maiden name was Sneyd, and this was given as a Christian name to the Davies's second son. Their first son, John, who died in 1735, aged 31, was, like Sneyd, well endowed with intellect and an amiable character, and was greatly mourned by his family. Both he and his mother were buried at Kingsland. Honora is said to have been 'greatly distinguished by her piety and charity'.

Sneyd was sent to Eton, where he became acquainted with Charles Pratt, later Lord Camden, and Frederick Cornwallis, who later became Archbishop of Canterbury. They remained his life-long friends.

When John Davies died in 1732 he left Sneyd the advowson of Kingsland; thus Sneyd Davies, who had just taken his first degree at King's College, Cambridge, became his successor as rector of Kingsland. In 1734 he obtained his

M.A., and, like his friend, Charles Pratt, became a Fellow
of his college. When Cornwallis became Bishop of Lichfield
in 1749 he appointed Sneyd to a chaplaincy. In 1751 he
made him Master of St. John's Hospital and Prebendary of
Lichfield, and in 1755 Archdeacon of Derby. Though he is
said to have been unambitious, he showed some irritation
when Pratt, as Attorney General in 1757–62 and as Lord
Chancellor in 1766, failed to obtain any patronage for him.
He acquired his D.D. in 1759.

Davies was a poet of no mean ability. He started writing
poetry when at school and continued throughout life to
contribute to various anthologies the fruits of his erudition
and talent. He became known in the literary circles of
Lichfield, and the famous letter-writer, Miss Anna Seward of
Lichfield, then a girl, 'wept tears of delight' at his earnest
and tremulous voice, and thought him a spirit 'beautified
before his time'.

In Timothy Thomas, the rector of Presteigne, he found a
fellow spirit. The two amused themselves by translating into
Latin verse Pope's 'Essay on Man', which, in the spirit of the
Enlightenment they clearly admired.

In those days various borderland gentlemen used to meet
annually on Caer Caradoc to celebrate the memory of the
valiant British chieftain, Caractacus. At one of these meetings
Sneyd Davies delivered, almost *ex tempore,* some animated
lines in honour of their hero. The following is an extract
from this poem:

> Brave Caradoc, applauded by thy foes,
> What shall thy friends, thy grateful Britons say?
> What columns, and what altars rear of fame?
> Thrice told five hundred courses of the sun,
> Thy age is green, thy laurels freshly bloom.
> Yet on thy well-fought hill, whose stony brow
> O'erlooks the subject plains, the gen'rous youth
> Gladsome repair with annual flow'rs and song,
> And festal music, to record thy praise.
> O for more sparks of thy heroic fire!
> If aught regarding this dull orb of earth,
> Boils not thy rage, and thy great spirit chafes,
> To see the rivals of all-conquering Rome,
> Thy hardy Britons, foil'd by tinsel France?

Imagination, frowning, pictures thee
With featur'd variations, scorn and shame.
Assist, inspire our host! But chiefly thou,
The champion, guardian-genius of this isle,
Hover around our tents; thy airy lance
Direct, and spread thy visionary shield!
Call, rouse thy countrymen! To arms, to arms.

For a great period of his life Dr. Davies, who never married, lived the life of a recluse in Kingsland, amusing himself by writing his poetry, corresponding with friends, and solacing himself with his books and his pipe. He is described as a man of most amiable character, simple, modest and unworldly.

He left his whole fortune, as well as the living of Kingsland, to Richard Evans who succeeded him as rector. He was buried at Kingsland on 26 January 1769.

Thomas George Hamilton-Baillie appears to have lived very extravagantly and to have entertained on a lavish scale. As a result he became involved in serious financial trouble, and had to leave the parish. During his stay in Kingsland the church was robbed of its precious pre-Reformation plate; the perpetrators of this theft were not detected and the plate never recovered. While the rector lived in exile from his parish, the work of the parish was carried out by a curate-in-charge. This was the Rev. James Jobling who carried out this function from 1896 until 1917 when he succeeded Hamilton-Baillie as rector. His son, George, followed him in the living. George Jobling knew his Kingsland well and wrote a short history of the parish, which, though unpublished and existing only in typescript, has proved valuable to the present writer.

Prebendary Herbert S. G. Thomas is remembered with affection and respect by all who knew him—by parishioners, perhaps, most of all, for he was indefatigable in their service, and many are the stories of his kindnesses to people in trouble. No inconvenience to himself was so great as to prevent him from solving the problems of those in need.

Like so many of the incumbents of Kingsland, Prebendary Thomas was an alumnus of Oxford, where he was a student of St. John's College, taking his first degree there in 1934.

Ordained deacon in 1935, he went as curate to Connah's
Quay in Flintshire. In 1936 he was ordained priest. He
joined the Forces as a chaplain in 1940, and he was attached
to the 4th Battalion, 'the Hallamshire Battalion', of the
York and Lancaster regiment, serving with it in Iceland and
Europe. He took part in the invasion of Normandy. He was
fearless in the battlefield, where he was often the first to
reach a soldier who had fallen. Brigadier T. Hart Dyke in his
Normandy to Arnhem (1966) wrote: 'Padre Thomas was
loved by all for his quiet Christian courage and his bravery
under fire, which later won for him the Military Cross', and
'He was a tower of strength'.

In 1946, on leaving the army, he was appointed vicar of
Kimbolton with Middleton-on-the-Hill and Hamnish. After
19 years' service to these parishes, he left his people there
with heavy hearts when the bishop instituted him rector of
Kingsland in 1965. In both spheres of activity he proved to
be the very pattern of an ideal parson, to whom Chaucer's
description of the 'Poure Persoun' in the Prologue of the
Canterbury Tales most aptly applies:

> Holy and virtuous he was, but then
> Never contemptuous of sinful men
> Never disdainful, never too proud or fine,
> But was discreet in teaching and benign.

The rector was a strong character, yet a most diffident
man. At his retirement on 31 October 1975, he made a
characteristic choice of a present—a bicycle. Much of his
visiting in the parishes he held had been done on his old
bicycle. He clearly intended to make use of the new one in
the place of his retirement, Condover in Shropshire.

The author was not surprised to discover that Prebendary
Thomas had a great reverence for, and devotion to, that
saintly French priest of the 19th century, the 'Blessed
Curé of Ars'.

Chapter Six

CATHOLIC RECUSANCY IN KINGSLAND

EVIDENCE WAS GIVEN on p. 25 that the Reformation had not affected Kingsland before the reign of Elizabeth. When the rector, Edmund Daniel, was ejected in 1559, he was succeeded by another priest who had been ordained in the reign of Henry VIII, but who was more willing to oblige the secular authority. His Protestant convictions were seemingly not very pronounced as he served Mary as willingly as Elizabeth.

There were a few people in Kingsland, however, who were not so compliant as their rector. These adhered to the old religion in spite of fines and persecution. In 1685 two families who had refused to conform received the general pardon extended by James II in that year to 'popish recusants'. These were the Colemans and the Pughs. Thomas Coleman and George Pugh had been summoned to take the oath of allegiance in 1678, the year of the notorious Oates 'plot'. Those granted the pardon of 1685 were Mary and Ann Coleman and George Pugh. As co-religionists and fellow sufferers they had as neighbours in Aymestrey the Bridge-waters, the Eales, the Everetts, the Garnons and the Ingrams; In Dilwyn, the Bowyers of Luntley Court; and, in Lucton, the important family of the Wigmores. Winifred Wigmore was one of the companions of Mary Ward, the foundress of the Institute of the Blessed Virgin Mary, and wrote the first life of that holy woman.

In his will of 1649 Cresacre More, the great-grandson and biographer of Sir Thomas More, refers to some property he had in Kingsland: 'Also I give to my said executors [viz. his cousins, Thomas Greenwood of Brise

33

Norton, Oxon. and William Roper, together with his friend
George Vaughan of Co. Monmouth and his old servant
Christopher Lewis] all that messuage and tenement with
the lands thereunto belonging . . . which I purchased of
Thomas Bull of Herton in the county of Hereford, Gent.
deceased lying in the parish of Kingsland co. Hereford and
now in the possession of Thomas Freeman or of his assigns'.

From the two entries in the registers of the parish church
in Kingsland it appears that in 1620-21 Cresacre More's
son, Thomas, was living in the parish:

'John, the sonne of Thomas Moore gent. was buried
20 Oct. 1620.'

'Elenor and Dorothie, the daughters of Thomas Moore
gent. were baptised 18th Dec. 1621.'

In the City Library, Hereford, there is preserved 'A List
of Papists within the County of Hereford, 1706'. Under
Kingsland it gives the names of Thomas Jenks, gent., John
Smith, cottager, and Elizabeth, the wife of Thomas Preece,
yeoman.

In 1767, however, the rector, Dr. Davies, and his curate,
Charles Morgan, were able to report to the bishop that
there were no papists in the parish. The vicar of Monkland
had to report one—Thomas Caldwall of Monkland Farm;
and Dilwyn regretfully admitted to two, the wife and
daughter of Lacon Lambe.

The Bowyer family appears to have at last conformed,
as did so many families in the 18th century. Lucton, too,
presented a clean sheet. The Wigmores had been forced to
sell their property in Lucton; it was already heavily mort-
gaged, the family having suffered greatly through their
lasting devotion to the Stuart cause. Robert Wigmore, who
was the last owner of the Lucton estate, had been pardoned
for his recusancy in 1685.

Chapter Seven

THE CHURCHWARDENS AND THEIR FUNCTIONS

A PERUSAL of the churchwardens' accounts now preserved in the County Record Office makes one aware of the many good works performed by these officers, and the heavy responsibility they bore. There were usually two, and they were elected for a year by the parish vestry. I have selected some items from these accounts to illustrate the work they did. To finance their many expenses they were allowed to levy a rate based on the land-tax paid by land-holders. This 'lewn', as it was called locally, varied with the demand in different years. The churchwardens had the job of collecting this sum, and the item 'uncollected dues' was usually remarkably small, in 1774 amounting to £2 16s. 11d. out of a total of about £87. The difference between the amount collected and that disbursed was often made up by several generous donors.

The chief work of the churchwardens was to maintain clean and in good repair the church, the clock, the church silver, and the one vestment of the clergyman, the surplice. They paid the parish clerk and the bell-ringers for special occasions, and found the bread and wine for the sacrament of Holy Communion at the festivals of Christmas, Easter, Whitsun and Michaelmas.

Just as important was their relief of the poor of the parish and passengers through it. They paid for the burial of paupers and acted as censors of behaviour. They 'presented' to the bishop lists of people who behaved in an unseemly or quarrelsome manner, or who absented themselves from church; such people were fined for each offence and, if wilfully 'recusant', they were excommunicated.

One painful duty incumbent upon the churchwardens was to discover the fathers of illegitimate children, and make them pay. They thus acted as constables. They paid people for catching and killing pests, and they were obliged to prepare and transmit to the bishop annually a 'transcript' of the church registers of baptisms, weddings and burials. Finally, they had expenses in connection with the 'visitation'. The bishop or archdeacon was expected to make a periodic inspection of the church, but the items in the churchwardens' accounts point to visits made by them to the ecclesiastical authorities, perhaps with their account books.

Selection of Items

1675		£	s.	d.
Bread and wine for Communion, Whitsun			4	4
Ale for 29th May			2	6
One bell rope			2	4
To Glazier for glazing in the church			9	8
Our expenses at the monthly meeting			1	0
Gave to a Blind man that came by				6
For four 75 foote of boards to make the church door			9	5
350 Nayles for the door			9	6
for the Hinges			4	8
for making 2 bolts			1	0
for make clean the clock and mending of him ..			3	2
two loads of tyle			7	0
carriage for same			8	0
for shingles			3	6
2 bushells of hair			1	0
2 horse loads of lime			3	4
to Tyler for tyling			17	0
nayles for the Tyler			1	0
ale for the Workmen in the Church			2	0
to Jane Barrar for mending the surplus				6
to Wm. Bedford (clerk) for his wages	1	0	0
to poor men (ten of them)			4	10
to a poore man that came with a pettison			1	6
1694 and Paid the first visitacion			6	10
1695 for ringing Nov. 5			2	6
for a book of thanksgiving			1	0
for a book to pray for the King				6
a book of Devotions			1	0

for the third visitacion		8	10
for the riting our presentment		1	0
for my Gorney to Hereford		2	0
Towling [tolling] for the Queen		1	0
for a poor whomans burriall		4	0
for sending the transcript			6
for going to Leominster the last visitacon		2	0
Paid to passingers 6d., 1s. 6d., 1s. 6d., 6d., 4d. ..		4	4

1706 For our charges to the Visitation at Hereford and
our dinners 4 0
delivering the presentment and for a prayer book
for the thanksgiving 5 10
paid to Walter Lugger for killing 6 urchings ..   1 0
for a Warrand for Serching for Stones that were
lost   6
Charges with the Warrand 1 0
to John Pember for menting of rack wheels of the
clock 1 0
for writing of the Lewn and the Account 15 0
paid to Ringers 6th Feb., Queen Anne's Birthday   2 6

1741 This year 28 urchins were caught by 9 catchers some
bringing only one.
a man was paid 1s. for killing 7 foxes.
Writing the Transcript 2 6
Parchment for it 1 0
For taking Transcript to Office 2 6
For entering into the Register.. .. .. ..   2 6
for cleaning the snow out of church.. .. ..   1 0
a ladder 7 6

1753 12 yards of Holland for the surples 1 16 0

Chapter Eight

RELIEF OF THE POOR

IN THESE EARLIER accounts the amounts of money paid to the poor of the parish are trifling, but as the 18th century advanced the work of the churchwardens as Poor Law Officers became ever more onerous, and the amounts levied for the relief was assessed at 6d. in the pound, and amount disbursed totalled £93 7s. 2d. The rates were as follows in successive years:

1774, 6d.; 1775, 1s. 6d.; 1776, 1s. 3d.; 1777, 1s. 6d.

1779	2s. 6d.	Disbursements this year	..	.. £120	4	4
1781	2s. 6d.	Disbursements this year	..	.. £151	11	2
1784	2s. 6d.	Disbursements this year	..	.. £140	17	1
1787	2s. 3d.	Disbursements this year	..	.. £124	0	0

In 1795 Assessments were made half-yearly:
    First half-year, 3s.; second, 4s.
    The lewn for 1796 amounted to £235 5s. 5d.

Before this time the problem of relieving the poor had become so great that for economy's sake poor people were no longer given 'out-relief', but were herded into a poor house. In 1784 Edward Stevens 'takes unto him the Poor of the Parish of Kingsland at 2s. 6d. in the £1 rate according to the Land Tax. He agrees to pay all County Rates and to do his endeavour to take hold of all Fathers of Bastard Children to be brought to justice, and that all children that are thought proper to be put out Apprentices are to be taken from him and put to proper places at the said Edw. Stevens' expenses'.

This housing of the poor was undertaken by John Gethin for the years 1789-1792. (In 1846, another John Gethin is described as the Guardian of the Union for the parish of Kingsland.)

In the 19th century the poor house in Kingsland became unnecessary, for the parish now shared the Leominster Union Workhouse, and paid for its inmates there.

Chapter Nine

NONCONFORMITY IN KINGSLAND

WE HAVE SEEN that the 'popish' recusants had disappeared from Kingsland by the middle of the 18th century. It is unlikely that all the tradesmen and farmers in Kingsland were now practising members of the Established Church, as most large parishes in Herefordshire had a Quaker or two, or a few Baptists, and Kingsland is unlikely to have been without a few dissenters.*

The first Protestant dissenters who were numerous enough in Kingsland to require their own place of worship were the Wesleyans, who appear to have built their chapel on the site of the existing Methodist chapel.

The present 'neat and commodious' chapel was built for them in 1857 by Mrs. Holloway. It never had a resident minister, being a part of the Leominster Circuit and was thus served ministerially from Leominster. Most of its services were conducted by lay preachers, among whom Mr. Small, a 'grand old man' and a 'comfortable speaker' was very prominent. When he died on 17 February 1933, aged 97, he was buried with his wife Ellen beside the chapel he had served for so long. The two are the only occupants of the chapel's graveyard. Another much loved and respected man was Mr. Edwin (Ted) Passey, who in 1900 passed his examination to become a lay preacher, and had served the Kingsland chapel since 1913; he became chapel steward and treasurer in 1921. Other frequent preachers were Mr. William Newman, Mr. A. Seale, and Mr. T. Richards. The chapel enjoyed its heyday about 50 years ago when it had between forty and fifty communicant members.

*In 1662 Richard Kennerdsley, his wife and daughter are reported as Quakers, not coming to church and not having their children baptised.

The Wesleyans developed a dissident group even in Kingsland. The 'Primitive Methodists' established their own chapel at Shirlheath in 1861.

The old-established Baptist chapel in Etnam Street, Leominster, acquired in 1883 a very active and popular minister in the Rev. W. H. Purchase. A Mr. Stevens and other Baptists who had settled in Kingsland begged him to conduct a Sunday afternoon service there. Once begun they continued with success, and in time a simple temporary chapel was erected, at small cost, because of the generous help given by Mr. Stevens and his friends. This was a wooden building in the garden of 'The Laurels', Longford. Baptisms at this period were carried out in the river Lugg at Lugg Green. In 1903 the permanent chapel was erected near the railway station.

In about 1900 the Moravians, who had long been established in Leominster, opened a mission room at Cobnash. Later, another chapel was called for, and a room was hired at Cholstrey, and while the Cobnash mission declined the one at Cholstrey flourished. Both are now closed and all trace of them has disappeared. The Cholstrey mission hall, however, was in use up to about 1960.

Chapter Ten

KINGSLAND CHARITIES

LIKE MOST ANCIENT PARISHES Kingsland has a lengthy list of benefactors. Christian charity never ceased to be practised, as the boards in churches recording bequests in favour of the poor remind us. Sadly, owing to inflation, gifts which once afforded substantial help to the needy are now worth little or nothing.

In 1697 Mary Barrar and others left £54 with which two pieces of land in the township of Aston were purchased. These were the 'Paddock' and the 'Hayes', which yielded £2 14s. 0d. per annum. In the early 19th century the church-warden distributed this with Morgan's Charity. (See p. 48)

A tablet in the church dated 1774 records that in 1726 John and Elizabeth Hood gave land (then vested in Thomas Hill, and producing 12s. per annum), for teaching two poor children. John Hood also left £10, the interest from which was to be paid regularly by his executor, Mr. John Burgin. In 1726, too, Richard Cutler and Timothy Matthews are said to have given by deed land producing 10s. per annum, to be paid out in bread for the poor.

The Charity Commissioners, however, found that the tablet was incorrect. No land was given either by John and Elizabeth Hood or by Cutler and Matthews, but the former gave £12 and the latter £10, which sums were laid out in the purchase of land: three acres in Lawton's Field and one acre in the Great West Field. From these the rector and churchwardens and overseers of the poor were to receive 10 shillings per annum to distribute to the poor. From 1822 the charge had not been collected; up to that date a Mr. Thomas Hill had paid, but his son failed to keep it up. When

reminded of this by the Commissioners, he consented to pay
the charges in the future on condition that his arrears were
excused. He promised to pay the rector 22s. at Christmas
in 1837, and to pay the same sum annually, half at Mid-
summer and half at Christmas.

The 1774 tablet also recorded that Mrs. Morgan of
Henblas, Anglesea, left £100 with which a piece of land
called Kinden Croft was purchased (1770).* The land was
to be let for the best rent obtainable, and the yield was to
be used for the maintenance and support of the poor. It was
to aid those sums which were from time to time assessed,
levied and raised by the town for the relief of the poor.
(This seems a short-sighted policy, for it would tend to make
the overseers less demanding on the ratepayers, the poor in
no way benefiting.) The land was let in 1831 for £10 10s. 0d.
The Commissioners found that no proper accounts had been
kept, except on loose pieces of paper; consequently the
minister and churchwardens undertook to keep a proper
account book, and to distribute the charities otherwise than
in small sums.

In his will of 1744 Benjamin Randell left £10, the interest
on which was to accumulate until a piece of land could be
purchased with it. Benjamin Randell junior died in 1794
leaving £10 to purchase land for the use of the poor. The
commissioners found that the executors had for several
years refused to pay the interest, the bequest being void
under the Mortmain Act.

In a will of 1810 Thomas Woodhouse gave and bequeathed
to the Rev. Richard Davies Evans and Edward Evans of
Eyton Hall £200 to be invested for the provision of education for the poor children of Kingsland. The trustees were
from time to time to employ a proper instructor for the
poor children, and pay him a reasonable salary out of the
dividends and interest of the sum twice a year. Another
bequest was made to be invested, and from the interest
on this bread was to be purchased and distributed to the

---

*The Croft had been enclosed out of a common field called Kin-
don's Field in the Manor of Kingsland. (Indenture of 1770, Hereford
C.R.O.).

poor of Kingsland on St. Thomas's Day, Easter Monday and Michaelmas Day 'in each year, for ever'.

In 1882 Miss Mary Roberts of Kingsland left the sum of £100 to be invested in the names of the rector and church-wardens in the 3 per cent. Consuls. The interest was to be expended in coals to be given to the poor of the parish.

Lucton Grammar School

The parish of Kingsland is entitled to a share in the Lucton Grammar School Charity founded in 1708 by John Pierre-pont, a wealthy London vintner, whose family were of Lucton. Other parishes having shares in the charity are Lucton, Croft, Yarpole, Bircher, Luston, Eyton, Shobdon and Aymestrey. To qualify for entrance to the school the 50 boys from these parishes or townships had to be able to read distinctly the Lord's Prayer, the Ten Commandments, the Creed, and a chapter of the New Testament. No boy was to be selected who was not sound and wholesome and free from any noisome infirmity, from any running sore or infectious disease. The parents of these boys were to be labourers or freeholders who had property worth £20 per annum or less, or who managed land at the same time of the yearly value of £50 or less.

Up to thirty more boys could be accepted whose parents owned or managed lands above the annual value of £50, but did not have in their own right lands or hereditaments above the yearly value of £50; or, either together with or without their own estate, did not rent or manage lands above a yearly value of £100.

Chapter Eleven

THE EDUCATION OF CHILDREN IN KINGSLAND

THE CHILDREN of the village of Kingsland did not lack the opportunity for an elementary education, even before the Reformation, for charitable persons had given land and tenements to maintain two priests to serve the chantry of Our Lady, one of whom taught the children. A survey made in 1547 records that '"Sir" John Hartley, of good conversation, aged 42, who celebrates, helps the curate, keepeth a school and doth bring up youth virtuously, and hath the clear revenue and profit of his scholars'.[1] (The title 'Sir' was applied to priests of that period. The 'curate' was the parish priest, or rector.)

It is possible that after this period the rector's curate was expected to conduct this small school as one of his duties, for it is reported that a school was held in the porch or vestry of the church before the building of a schoolhouse in 1846.[2] In the chapter concerning charities we note that in 1810 Thomas Woodhouse had provided funds for the education of the poor children of Kingsland (by these, one presumes he meant those whose parents could not afford the normal fees). In founding Lucton school in 1708, John Pierrepont provided for the secondary education of some Kingsland boys, so their elementary education was probably obtained in the village school.

Great social changes accelerated by the French Revolution and the Industrial Revolution, resulting in a popular demand for electoral rights, highlighted the need for more general education. The rivalry between the Established Church and the numerous Protestant dissenters led to their championing the cause of education and establishing schools which endeavoured to instil in the pupils, in addition to the '3 Rs', the principles of those who found the money to build and maintain the schools. In supporting the British and Foreign Schools' Society (founded in 1814), and being of many differing views, the Nonconformists were content to give an undenominational Christian education. The National Schools Society (founded in 1811) existed to give an Anglican education. Kingsland, being small, could not support more than one school, so the Nonconformists had either to send their children to the church school, or to the distant British school in the Bargates, Leominster.

Kingsland's schoolhouse was opened by the rector's wife on 26 October 1846. It cost only £262 10s. 0d. some of which was contributed by the National Schools Society. The stone for its construction was given by Mr. B. Sanders of Street Court, and hauled from the quarry on his estates by teams of volunteers from the village. The grateful rector, who gave a portion of the Glebe land for the site of the building, compiled a list of their names in the church register. The erection of the school is an event which Kingsland people should be proud of, for it was an effort shared by most of the inhabitants. Let us hope that in these days when village schools are so often closed in the name of economy or efficiency, this school will continue.

NOTES

1. In a document of 1557 'le Scholehouse' is mentioned as belonging to the chantry.

2. The upper part of the vestry was added in the 15th century, and the upper room thus formed is said to have served as the schoolroom. The floor of this room has been removed, raising the height of the vestry ceiling.

Chapter Twelve

THE ANNUAL FAIR

THE ANNUAL FAIR which used to be held on 'Fair Field' (the large field near the church) on the feast day of St. Michael, the church's patron (old Michaelmas Day, 11 October) is as old as the present church, and dates from the reign of Edward I. It was granted by Margaret, the widow of Lord Mortimer, *c.* 1305. Animals sent to the fair were 'tolled' by wardens who occupied cottages at the principal approaches to the village, to the north and south. One cottage was called 'Upper Wardens', the other 'Lower Wardens'. The northern cottage stood where the Glendaph Nursing Home now stands. The site of 'Lower Wardens' has been forgotten. The fair was still being held in 1826, when it was called by the Welsh 'Fair Leonau'—'the Leon Fair'. Like the large church, it bears witness to a populous Kingsland in the late 13th century. The village was still populous at the end of the Middle Ages, for the survey of King Edward VI already quoted gives the number of 'Houseling' people as 300.

Chapter Thirteen

FORMER OCCUPATIONS OF KINGSLAND FOLK

THOUGH KINGSLAND has never become a town its inhabitants have practised many skills beside that of farming. A bailiff's account surviving from the year 1389-90 mentions officers such as bailiffs, stewards and reeves, and craftsmen such as carpenters and millers. There was, no doubt, always a smith, though he is not mentioned. What is surprising at this date is that beside water corn-mills there was also a fulling-mill, which was worked by one Richard Walker. Now a 'walker' was a man who 'fulled' cloth by 'walking' it, or pounding it with feet, or hands, to 'thick' or felt it, for the purpose of making hats. Thus it would appear that hats or caps were made in Kingsland at that time, as they were later in Leominster. On the other hand, the Kingsland fuller may have made felt for the Leominster hat- and cap-makers. The two other water-mills are named in the document as Oxenfordemulle and Lorkenmulle. A further mill, at that time undergoing repair, was 'in Okere', presumably Oaker Wood. For the repair of mills timber was felled in the Lord's wood at 'Henton' (Hinton), which was then, and continued to be, a distinct manor until 1929, when John Paton was its lord.

The making of mead from honey, ale from barley, and cider from apples must have been practised in Kingsland since time immemorial. Cider was brewed up to the 19th century, and when work had to be done at a distance from home the cider was carried by the worker in little oak barrels commonly called 'costrels', but known in the Kingsland area as 'bottles'. These generally held about a gallon, but there were smaller ones; a woman's bottle was much smaller and rarely held more than a third of the quantity allowed

48

for a man. Most of these costrels were made by a Kingsland cooper.

In connection with cider-making, I must quote my informant, the late Rev. George Jobling.

> Once the fruit had been crushed in the circular trough of the cider-mill it was spread thickly between 'hairs', and layers of these thick blankets were placed on top of each other in a large press. This arrangement not only produced the necessary juice, but also kept back the solid matter, and filtered the juice at the same time. The refuse was then thrown out and fermented, the result being that when the pigs fed upon it, they became quite drunk and staggered about until they could sleep it off. This heavily fermenting refuse (called 'must') was once eaten by ducks at Cobnash. The owner found them apparently dead on the snow and plucked them for the Leominster market. The hard frost outside had been partly responsible for the birds' collapse, so that when in the house before the warm fire, they began to revive. Several had already been plucked. To save their lives, the poor woman made for them scarlet woollen coats, which they wore till the thaw came and their feathers began to grow again.

(The Must mill, still surviving as a building, must have contained a cider-mill.).

The Bone mill (now a private house renamed 'Kingsfield') at O.S. 435 623 was used to grind bones to make phosphatic fertiliser for the fields, and in 1858 Henry Fowler was making bone-meal there. Like most mills it may have been used for other purposes in the past. Mills for fulling and paper-making were usually converted corn-grinding mills. Paper-making was carried out at the Mortimer's Cross mill in the 18th century.

Having two swiftly-flowing rivers in its vicinity, Kingsland was always well-off for mills. Where the Oxenforde and Lork mills of medieval times were we can only guess; they were perhaps the two mills mentioned in the Domesday Survey. One was undoubtedly Kingsland mill on the Lugg at O.S. 448 622. The Day House mill, nearby at O.S. 446 623 appears to have been there for centuries. The Bone mill was worked by Lugg water, and the Must mill by a leet from the Pinsley. The Pinsley also supplied the water for the Waterloo mill (O.S. 452 605) whose huge wheel was made at the

Leominster foundry of Miles in 1881, though this replaced
an earlier wheel. The name of the mill suggests 1815 as the
date of construction, which seems likely, for corn was
fetching a high price during the Napoleonic Wars, and local
farmers took advantage of this fact and grew as much as
they could. The mill was still in operation in 1900 when a
Mr. Edward Hellaby owned the mill and the farm attached.
In the township of Lawton, Arrow mill (O.S. 436 587)
was still working in 1900 when it was owned by Thomas
and William Davies, and drew its water from the river Arrow.

Glove-making, so important an industry in Leominster
early in the 19th century, was also practised in Kingsland.
The Must mill, once so attractive with a thatched roof, was
at about the same period a glove factory. In 1841 Philip
Postans was a tailor, and in 1858 Kingsland had in James
Scandrett of Brook Bridge (O.S. 432 615) a tailor and
draper. Physicians and veterinary surgeons also seem for
a long time to have made a living in Kingsland and its
neighbourhood.

As late as 1925 G. Lewis and Son were making the
'Convertible Jubilee Wagon' and the Herefordshire 'Prize
Medal' carts at the premises now renamed 'The Garth'
opposite the school. This firm also acted as Kingsland's
undertakers.

In 1857 Kingsland had its own basket-maker in the person
of John Hornsby.

We know the names of at least two postmen, John Sankey
and following him, his son, Charles Sankey, who also practised the trade of saddler. John and his wife Mary were living
at Shirlheath when Charles was born in 1865. Still preserved
in the Sankey family, of which four generations of boys
attended Lucton school, is the post horn which John blew
at the crossroads to summon people to bring their letters
and to collect any he had for them.

In 1858, six miles of the river Lugg were reserved as a
fishery, and the conservator was Richard Williams of Kingsland, who manufactured fishing-tackle.

As the 20th century has advanced the crafts of Kingsland's
inhabitants have gradually disappeared, owing to the

KINGSLAND, R.S.O.,

Herefordshire,

Established over
Half a Century.

Dec   *192ᵔ5*

To The Exocors of the late
Mr Mrs Price. Holgate /Kingsland

DR. TO **G. LEWIS & SON,**

Makers of the Convertible Jubilee Wagon and the Herefordshire Prize Medal Carts.

UNDERTAKERS.   *£ s d.*

Letterhead of G. Lewis & Son, 1925

adoption of new ways of life and the competition of mass-producers. The population still has its agriculturalists, but it tends to consist of commuters working further afield, and of retired people seeking a quiet life in a beautiful and healthy environment.

Chapter Fourteen

INNS

INNS HAVE LOST one of the important functions which they performed in earlier times. For centuries they were meeting places to which men resorted to transact business during markets and fairs. An inn was usually also the place in which the court leet and parish vestry met. Though, no doubt, much 'shop' is still talked in public houses, this aspect of their existence is not now very prominent, and it is therefore not surprising that fewer are needed.

It is agreeable to report that Kingsland's most ancient inn, the *Angel,* is open again after a period when it had no licence. It is the Kingsland inn *par excellence* because it is named after the church's patron, St. Michael, and it is very near to the church. Next door is the 'Angel House' (O.S. 447 613) which was probably the original hostelry. When it was being restored some years ago by Captain Hamlen Williams, some stone used in its construction was noticed to be of the same kind as was used for building the church. Perhaps the earliest *Angel* was contemporary with the church. Another interesting discovery made during this restoration was that of a great fireplace hidden behind a lath-and-plaster wall. The chimney-piece of white oak was adorned with Tudor roses burnt into the wood with a brand from the fire. The legend arose that these were made by some soldiers whiling away the time while on guard outside the bedroom of one of the captains on the night before the battle of Mortimer's Cross. Sadly, this is unlikely to be true because fireplaces against walls and chimney-stacks did not come into use before the 16th century. In any case, the rose adornments were obliterated by the ignorant workmen in their anxiety to improve the house's appearance. R.C.H.M. dates the 'Angel House' to the late 16th century.

The *Corners,* a very flourishing public house at the crossing at O.S. 445 616, is another fine timber-framed building which has been considerably altered and extended since it was first built (probably in the late 16th century).

Opposite to the 'Croase House' at the same crossroads stands the former *Bell* inn; the bell of the sign can still be discerned painted on the south-east wall. This inn was called the *Blue Bell* in 1886.

The *Red Lion,* near the sharp bend in the road at O.S. 453 609, fairly recently became a private house.

The *Monument* at the road fork O.S. 437 619 takes its present name from the memorial to the battle of Mortimer's Cross which stands outside it. The inn was called *The Horseshoes* in 1900, and in 1801 *The Mortimer's Cross.*

Another inn which has disappeared was the *Dog,* the name of which survives in Dog Lane between Lawton and Cobnash. There was also the *Crown* inn at Shirl Heath in 1858.

Chapter Fifteen

ROADS, CANAL AND RAILWAY

Roads

KINGSLAND was on the coaching road from London to Aberystwyth, a distance of 214 miles which was covered in 24 hours. In 1800 a map shows the main road from Bromyard to Presteign passing through Leominster and the centre of Kingsland. C. Smith's map of Herefordshire of 1808 shows the road branching left at a public house called the *Mortimer's Cross* (now the *Monument*), and going directly to Shobdon and continuing through Presteign to New Radnor and Aberystwyth. It must be remembered, however, that in 1800 Aberystwyth was not the important place it has since become. William Hutton, who visited it in 1797, says 'It seems to contain about 200 houses' and 'it should only be seen at a distance, for the streets are miserable'.

An Act to set up turnpikes in the neighbourhood of Leominster, which provided for the improvement of the roads through Kingsland, Eardisland and Monkland and which was passed in 1729, explained why these provisions were necessary:

These roads 'by reason of the deep Soil thereof, and the heavy Carriages passing through the same, are become so ruinous and bad, that in the Winter Season many parts thereof are impassable for Waggons and Carriages, and also for Horses laden, and other parts are dangerous to Travellers'.

Canals

In 1790 the Earl of Oxford, Viscount Bateman, the Rt. Hon. Thomas Harley, and other interested gentlemen met at

54

Kington to discuss the building of a canal between Kington and Leominster. This canal was to join another which was to connect Leominster to Stourport on the Severn. The projected waterway between Kington and Stourport never materialised, though in 1796 a section of it was completed between Leominster and Mamble, which made possible the transport of coal from the nearby colliery of Sir Walter Blount to Leominster. In 1795 a start was made on the Kington to Leominster section near Kingsland, where about a mile of the 'cut' was dug in the Great West Field, and where traces of it can still be found (across a field north of the road junction at the *Monument*, and bordering a field south-west of the Day House). The foundations of an aqueduct over the river Lugg had been started.

In 1803 the engineer, John Hodgkinson, suggested that tramroads could be constructed much more cheaply than canals, and that such a railroad should be built between the canal wharf at Leominster and Kington. In August of that year an Act was passed authorising the construction of these tramroads. This plan appears later to have been abandoned (but *see under* 'Railway').

In 1811 a decision was made 'to continue the line of the canal from Leominster to Kingsland Field'. In the same year it was proposed that a tramroad or a canal should be built to connect the canal near Orleton, through Yarpole and Kingsland, with the Lugg at Mortimer's Cross; but both these schemes came to nothing.

(*See also* C. Hadfield, *The Canals of South Wales and the Border*, 1900.)

Railway

It was the building of the railways which led to the disuse of the canals. A railway or tramway for the use of horse-drawn trams conveying heavy freight, such as stone, lime, coal and timber between Kington and Leominster was projected before 1830. This track, with a gauge of 3ft. 6ins., was constructed from Kington to Eardisley, and served a useful purpose for some years. Lewis's *Topographical*

Dictionary certainly anticipated its completion to Leominster in 1831, for of Eardisland we read the following, 'The railroad from Kington to Leominster passes through it'.

When the steam locomotive superseded the horse as a means of traction, the railway age had set in. The line between Kington and Leominster was commenced on 30 November 1854, and its whole length was opened for transport in 1857. It remained in use for passenger transport until 1955 and for freight for another nine years; the last train ran on the line in September 1964. The station buildings and the level-crossing houses in Kingsland have now been converted into substantial dwellings.

Chapter Sixteen

KINGSLAND, A CENTRE OF DRAMATIC ART

FOR OVER 40 YEARS after 1880 a number of enthusiastic people made Kingsland well known in Herefordshire as a centre of amateur dramatic performances. They began without any intention of forming a permanent company by acting short plays to raise money to relieve the distress of the poor of the parish. At first they used the schoolroom as their theatre, but soon found the large room in the barn at the 'Croase House' more suitable for their large audiences. This was put at their disposal by Dr. Williams, whose wife, after overcoming a good deal of initial shyness, became an enthusiastic actress. Her example attracted the vicar's wife, Mrs. Bradley, to do the same, and Dr. Williams himself occasionally took a part. The upper part of the magnificent old barn made an excellent theatre, although with its thatched roof, uneven floor and difficult stairs it gave its owner much anxiety on account of the possibility of fire. Dr. Williams was unremitting in his vigilance, and no untoward incident occurred at the Croase during its long service as a theatre.

In those days stages were illuminated by oil lamps, rehearsals were difficult to arrange—there were no telephones in houses—and long journeys had to be made in winter over roads we would now regard as atrocious. Instead of cars people used slow and cumbersome brakes. Furthermore, at that time it was still thought slightly improper for a lady to take part in a stage play. However, the absence of motor transport did not keep people away, for on one occasion five hundred tried to obtain admission to the Croase room, spectators being crowded as far as the stairs.

The plays acted were light and humorous with a popular appeal; there were usually two short pieces. The first evening set the general tone with *The Area Belle* and *Cox and Box*. Other titles were *The Lottery Ticket, Freezing a Mother-in-Law, A Phenomenon in a Smock Frock,* and *The Virginian Mummy* (a Negro farce). The plays came to an end in 1903 with *Ici on parle Francais, Caste* and *Two Heads are Better than One,* but concerts continued until 1933, though these were usually performed in the schoolroom.

In the admirable tradition of this home-made entertainment the money raised was used for many charitable purposes: for the poor, for the organ fund, for the church bells and church restoration fund, for a children's treat, and for the Farmers' Benevolent Association, for example.

Chapter Seventeen

THE FIRE BRIGADE

FROM 1893, when Mrs. Price of 'Stanley Villa' presented the village with its first fire-engine, until the World War of 1939, the parish had a fire brigade consisting entirely of volunteers. Its captain for 35 years was Dr. Robert Williams of the 'Croase House'. The fire-engine was housed in a shed on his premises, and each year he and Mrs. Williams entertained the firemen to a special supper. In 1928 Dr. Williams resigned as captain in favour of his nephew, Mr. A. H. Williams of Holgate Farm, and became the brigade's honorary secretary. In 1937 the management committee of this efficient brigade consisted of the above, together with Mr. F. J. Colebatch, Mr. J. C. Price and Captain D. W. Hamlen Williams.

In 1927 it was felt that the old horse-drawn pump should be replaced by a modern steam pump which could be towed by a lorry, lent by a local man who owned three. He declared that one of his lorries was always ready and available for emergencies. The new pump was purchased with money saved by good management from charges made for services; the sum ran to three figures, and the little extra required for the purchase was raised by a few voluntary efforts. The brigade was proud to be no burden on the rates.

With the new engine no delay occurred in getting up steam. The fire under the boiler was not lit until the brigade was within four minutes of its destination. Steam was obtained in seven minutes, thus three minutes were allowed for coupling up. Using a one-inch jet this engine could throw water to a height of 120ft.; when four half-inch jets were fitted and used together the water was projected 90ft.

Chapter Eighteen

POPULATION

THE POPULATION of Kingsland seems to have remained fairly constant, though the proportion of young people must have declined considerably in recent years as more and more retired people have discovered its charms and taken up residence there.

According to the Chantry certificate for Herefordshire of 1548 (E. 301/24) there were in that year 300 'housling people' in Kingsland (figures are not given for Eardisland or Monkland). For comparison, there were 1,750 in Hereford, 1,800 in Leominster, 380 in Weobley, 500 in Pembridge, and 300 in Dilwyn.

Census figures are not available before 1831, when the number of inhabitants was 989. Since then the following figures have been given:

1851, 1,135; 1871, 1,138; 1891, 975; 1901, 910; 1911, 944; 1921, 901; 1931, 914; 1951, 911; 1961, 848; 1971, 850.

Kingsland did not escape its catastrophes in the past. From the church register of burials the number of deaths in the 16th century varied as a rule between nil and 10 per annum, but in 1546 the number rose to 19, and in 1551 to 26 (this was probably due to the plague).

The number of illegitimate children born and baptised in Kingsland reveals that this is not a feature unique to our age, but the number of illegitimate births must have reached an all-time high in 1804, when 6 out of 36 baptisms were of 'base-born' children.

The following figures, which are averages of 10 years at the beginning of each century, reveal that the birth-rate always exceeded the death-rate, so that if the population remained roughly stable some of the villagers must have migrated to other places. The low marriage rate appears to confirm this.

	Baptisms	Burials	Weddings
c. 1600 p.a.	11	8	3
c. 1700 p.a.	14	11	2
c. 1800 p.a.	29	19	7

Chapter Nineteen

PERSONALITIES

Some Distinguished Former Inhabitants

TWO FAMILIES of Kingsland recur in the registers for centuries, namely the Colemans and the Luggers. Both names occur in the bailiff's accounts for 1390. The families intermarried, and we find Coleman-Lugger unions in 1542, 1613 and 1617. We have noticed the Colemans as recusants in 1678 and 1685; the Luggers often served as churchwardens and one of them, a John Lugger, was good enough to transcribe the earliest registers. In doing so he showed his pride in his forebears by making Lugger entries very prominent. The family reached its apotheosis when one of their number served at Court, as these entries prove:

> John Lugger, yeoman Waytor of the Tower in ordinary to king James of his guard extraordinary and Elizabeth the daughter of Thomas Grismond married 1 Feb. 1624.
>
> 1626. John the sonne of John Lugger yeoman Waytor of ye Tower in ordinary to King James and of his Guard extraordinary was baptised 8 Oct.

Both families were numerous, but the Luggers seem to have lived for a long time at the Malthouse, and the Colemans at Lawton.

Colemans and Luggers also intermarried with Addises, another once prominent Kingsland family. At the Hereford County Record Office there is an indenture of 1631 made between John Lugger of Kingsland (surely the 'Yeoman Waytor') and John Addis of Kingsland which refers to 'lands in occupation of Thomas Moore, Gent.'. (See page 34)

We know from other sources that Thomas, the son of Cresacre More of Madley, married Mary, daughter of Sir

Basil Brook; their third son, Basil, was Thomas's heir. Was this the Bazill Moore of Kingsland who undertook, in 1681, to supply four yards of the churchyard wall, while John Coleman promised two yards? (*See* churchwarden's accounts.)

The Kingsland Wonder-Worker: Elizabeth Hughes

At Kingsland church on 5 December 1793 John Hughes, a poor husbandman, married Elizabeth Turner, a widow who had been born on a farm in Bodenham in about 1755. Both were unable to sign their names. Elizabeth was destined to make Kingsland nationally famous, for just after 1800 she gained a great reputation as a wonder-worker, and became known as the 'Kingsland Doctress'. A correspondent to the *Gentleman's Magazine*, Mr. J. P. Malcolm, who paid a visit in 1804 to the Hughes's farm at Fowden, described how this came about.

In June 1802 (Malcolm's '1803' has been corrected by the church register) one of the twins born to John and Elizabeth died. The mother was deeply afflicted 'and her lamentations were excessive: however in the midst of them she was not deprived of sleep; and very profitable dreams were afforded her. One of these exhibited an angel to her ken, who brought her the deceased child, which she nursed with great affection for an hour. This vision made a great impression on her mind, and introduced a long train of reflections, which at length terminated in a persuasion that she was a great sinner, with whom the Divinity was greatly displeased. To appease this displeasure, Elizabeth resolved upon repentance and prayer; and this was effected in solitude and privacy, to so much purpose that a second vision ensued by which she was acquainted that she might perform miracles in the cure of lameness, blindness and all morbid afflictions'.

From then on she proceeded to lay her hands upon those who came to her with their complaints. She expected implicit faith from her clients, and it is obvious that many went away believing themselves cured, for her reputation grew to such an extent that poor and rich came from near and far to experience the effect of her prayer and the touch of her

hands. Waggons and carriages from places as far apart as
Portsmouth and Northallerton were seen passing through
Leominster on their way to the doctress of Fowden.

Elizabeth's success aroused the ire of the intellectuals of
the day, who were amazed at this 'recrudescence of medieval
superstition'. They were the heirs of the 18th-century
Enlightenment, which had had no room for miracles in its
perception of the universe. The men of those times had not
experienced the phenomenon of Lourdes, the effects of
Mary Baker Eddy's 'Christian Science' and the surprising
claims of faith healers generally. The intellectual climate
was against Elizabeth and she was roundly denounced as a
'vile imposter'. Thomas Howldy, a Hereford schoolmaster,
composed a satirical poem in rhyming couplets called 'The
Wonder of Wonders or the Woman of Kingsland' of which
I quote a few lines:

> I sing the wondrous Woman, at whose prayer
> And holy touch Diseases disappear.
> . . . . . .
> Know this, ye sons of Credulity, know
> 'Tis faith alone can conquer every woe!
> Have faith in Mrs. Hughes, to her abode,
> Sons of Affliction, flee by ev'ry road!
> After her touch and prayer, the wind and spasm
> No more shall trouble any—but he who has 'em!
> . . . . . .
> Bend your quick steps to Kingsland's idol, where
> You'll meet with wonders that are truly rare.

The author of the letter to the *Gentleman's Magazine*
was equally scornful. He believed Mrs. Hughes was merely
a hoaxer who was intent on making a fortune out of her
gross deception. He said she was either a stupid, deceived
fanatic, or one who richly deserved transportation.

Others declare that she charged nothing for her atten-
tions, though it may be that grateful patients occasionally
pressed money upon her children. Tradesmen of Kingsland
benefited, of course, and, in particular, the inn-keepers.
A baker is said to have charged visitors 6d. for a one-ounce

loaf and a small cup of perry, and one farmer charged visitors who took a short cut across his field. Who could expect otherwise?

Mrs. Hughes died in 1849. When recording her burial on 28 March 1849, the rector, R. D. Evans, added: 'Formerly a celebrated Charmer. Persons came from all parts to be cured of their diseases; About 45 years ago. A great imposter'.

But was she? In a long letter to the *Hereford Times*, dated 20 April 1849, and written from Leominster, but unsigned, the author, possibly the Quaker John Southall, says: '. . . as my memory extends back probably farther than that of many others of your correspondents, I venture to give to you a few stray remembrances on the subject; and truly Betty Hughes must be acknowledged to have been a remarkable person . . .

'The writer has a recollection of seeing Betty Hughes in 1805, and she appeared a respectable, matronly-looking countrywoman. That she was no mere mercenary or wilful imposter is, to my mind, satisfactorily proved by the circumstances of her having rejected the pecuniary gifts of her patients'.

Several people living in Kingsland today claim relationship to this remarkable woman. Mrs. Miles, formerly Miss Postans, tells how a grandmother or great-grandmother was suffering from 'white-leg', a disease which the doctor could not cure. Mrs. Hughes was brought to her and effected a cure, which quite amazed the medical man.

Dick of the Delf

In his notes on Kingsland, kindly lent to me by the late rector, the Rev. George Jobling, is told the following story of one of these strange characters who in a simpler England could pursue an almost independent existence.

'Pinsley rises in Shobdon Marshes, part of which are in the parish of Kingsland and at the edge of a wood which is called Marsh Cover. Considerable springs bubble up there into two small ponds called Lady Pools. These are not more than twenty feet across and are filled with clear water resting on what looks like clear sand, but of incredible depth. The "white sand" is really very thin peat held in suspension.

'There is a tradition that a man and his wife used to live in this marsh, his hovel being in the middle of the bog which was almost impenetrable in winter. He was called Dick of the Delf, and maintained himself and his family by keeping a cow and one or two sheep and pigs on the edge of the marsh and probably very extensive poaching.'

John Gethin, Bridge-Builder

The Gethin family seems to have become prominent early in the 19th century. The group of tombstones just east of the church is not only a witness to their prosperity, but to the fact that John, born in 1757, was apprenticed to a stonemason and became a master of his craft. He also had considerable mathematical ability, and he set up in business with his brother Benjamin.

The brothers had their first great opportunity when, in February 1795, the unusually heavy falls of snow suddenly melted after lying for two months. The rivers rose rapidly and the devastating flood did immense damage to Herefordshire bridges. It is reported that the Wye rose 15ft. in 24 hours. The arch and part of the pier of the old bridge at Aymestrey were carried away and the brothers Gethin were requested to rebuild it. They made so good a job of it that they secured contracts for the rebuilding of many more bridges. These bridges, built entirely with hand tools, are so solid that they have stood up well to 20th-century traffic, and attract the admiration of civil engineers.

While continuing his work as a bridge-builder, John Gethin was appointed as surveyor of all the Herefordshire bridges, c. 1800. He remained bridge inspector (a post which carried a salary of £101 per annum) until his death on 24 May 1831, aged seventy-three.

The Gethins did not only build and repair bridges; they undertook all sorts of building work and were, I am afraid, responsible for giving to many a timber-framed house a fashionable brick façade. Tastes have changed, and today we prefer to see the pattern of the brown, or black and white panelling of the earlier architecture.

John Gethin lived in the 'Brick House', though the family had much property in and around the village. Material at the County Record Office and in private hands shows that the Gethins were interested in 'Stone House' (Stonleigh), 'The Villa', Kingsland, Arrow and Waterloo mills, a farm at Cob Nash, and the *Angel* inn.

Dr. Robert Williams

Dr. Williams was born and died at the Croase in the heart of Kingsland. His work in connection with the dramatic society and the fire brigade has already been noticed, but he was above all a most popular and successful physician. He was born in 1849, the son of Thomas and Anne Williams of the Croase. His father is described as a yeoman, but other members of the family were 'farmers'. Robert was educated at Hereford Cathedral school and qualified at Edinburgh. For half a century he was Medical Officer at Leominster. He was interested in sport and was an expert at fishing. He was the founder of the Arrow Lodge of Freemasons at Kington, and was at one time Past Prov. Grand Officer of the Province of Herefordshire.

Dr. Williams's epitaph in the church sums up his life and character, but the memory of his many kindnesses lingers yet in the minds of the older inhabitants of Kingsland:

'Robert Williams, Beloved Physician, whose life was devoted to the service of his fellows and to the welfare of this village. He died Dec. 1936 in his 88th year at the Croase House where he was born.'

Richard Henry George

One of the oldest houses in Kingsland was from 1913 to 1922 the residence of Mr. R. H. George, who is chiefly remembered for his book, *A History of the Herefordshire Borderland*. When living at 'Upper House' (which he renamed

---

'Croft Mead'), he gave rein to his passion for antiquarian studies and produced the papers on local history which he delivered to the Leominster Literary Society and the Woolhope Club of Hereford. A collection of these was issued under the above title by the Orphans' Printing Press of Leominster in 1914.

Mr. George was a native of Bircher. As a youth he was articled to Messrs. Lythall and Mansell, auctioneers and estate agents of Shrewsbury. When qualified, he set up in business as an estate agent, auctioneer and valuer at Byecroft, Bircher. He prospered and acquired important agencies both locally and in Gloucestershire. His work gave him excellent opportunities to get to know the towns, villages and old houses of the Borderland, the history of which he never tired of reading and researching. He made a splendid collection of old books relating to Leominster, Ludlow and the Welsh Marches generally, and what he learnt he loved to share with others.

In 1905 Mr. George became a member of the Woolhope Club, of which he was elected vice-president in the years 1915, 1916, and 1917. He had considerable literary ability which found full scope in the papers he wrote.

He was one of the founder members of the Kingsland branch of the 'Comrades of the Great War', and he helped the movement by providing the 'Bungalow' as its headquarters.

He left Kingsland in about 1922 to live at 42 Burgess Street, Leominster. He died in the Cottage hospital of that town on 12 June 1928, aged 69 and was buried at Yarpole.

Henry Langford of Waterloo Mill

Henry Langford was born at Wellington, Herefordshire, in 1875, and came to Kingsland from Canon Pyon in 1908. He settled at Waterloo mill on the Pinsley brook as a farmer, miller and corn merchant.

Owing to considerable alterations in the water course, the mill was closed down in 1930. After that time the

Hereford *Directory* describes Henry Langford and Sons of Waterloo mill as 'Cider Makers'.

In politics he was a keen Liberal and a champion of the rights of working men, with whom he was very popular; he was also a great friend and supporter of Edmund Lamb, who was displaced as Liberal M.P. for Leominster in the election of 1910. Mr. Langford served as a county councillor from 1913 up to the time of his death in 1954. He also served on the Leominster Borough Council and was mayor of Leominster in 1945 and 1946.

Henry Langford was very blunt in expressing his views and often gave great offence to his political opponents; at times he even embarrassed his friends. This 'rough diamond', as he has been described, was no mean ornithologist, and is remembered with affection by relatives and friends.

Unpopular Millers provoke Riots

In December 1774 a number of people in north-west Herefordshire were so incensed against two millers that they gathered together and furiously attacked their water corn-mills. John Parry, the owner of Arrow mill, Kingsland, was the first object of their spite. About sixty men, women and children led by Charles Powell of Pembridge, 'feloniously and tumultuously' fell upon the mill, smashing mill hoppers, hoops, millstones, troughs and a dressing-mill chest. Furthermore, they destroyed the cloth for dressing flour and everything belonging to the dressing-mill; they broke the arms of two water-wheels, destroyed three bushels of wheat and did further damage to the mill and mill-house. This attack was made on 12 December.

On 16 December, James Parry, a labourer of the parish of Monnington, and about thirty others perpetrated a similar attack on two mills operated by Edward Jones of Monnington. In his deposition, Jones stated that they broke two mill troughs, two mill hoppers, five ladles, two arms, two pens, one French stone, and destroyed nine dressing cloths at the first mill. Later the same day they began to demolish another mill of his, smashing two mill troughs, two mill hoppers, two mill hoops, five ladles, three arms, one French stone, and destroying nine dressing cloths.

By 1 February 1775, the ringleaders were rounded up and committed to gaol in Hereford. The two mentioned in the newspaper report of 2 February, as being committed by the Rev. John Woodcock. D.D., were Thomas and James Parry 'for pulling down a set of mills' belonging to John Parry of Kingsland and Edward Jones of Monnington. These men appear to have been regarded as heroes by many of their fellow countrymen, for *Pugh's Hereford Journal* of 9 February 1775 reports that 'a number of people from the country, amongst whom were some colliers, assembled in a tumultuous manner at the outer door of the gaol on Monday evening, and demanded the release of the two prisoners; which not being complied with, they began with sledge hammers to batter down the gaol door. Some gentlemen of the city, from a motive of humanity, mixed in the crowd, and remonstrated to them the ill consequences that would attend so daring an attempt, but all to no purpose. Our worthy and vigilant Chief Magistrate immediately assembled the civil power, and with several of the principal inhabitants proceeded towards the gaol, and caused the riot act to be read twice, during which time the rioters had forced the outer door of the goal, when several firearms were discharged from within, by which one man was shot dead on the spot, and several others wounded'. This had a sobering effect on the others, so that they soon dispersed, threatening, however, to return in larger numbers. They were obviously cowed, for they did not return, and the city patrols were able to relax their vigilance.

At the March assizes James Parry, Thomas Parry, Charles Powell and Thomas Gumner (Gunther, Gummer) were sentenced to death for pulling down and destroying corn mills. The sentence was 'Guilty to be hanged. No good'. Ali four were later reprieved. For some unspecified reason, Charles Powell received a free pardon; the sentence on the others was commuted to transportation for 14 years to plantations in America. James Parry was regarded as the worst offender, for he was the last to obtain a reprieve. The story was not yet over, for in April, as Thomas Parry, together with four others, was being escorted to the port for transportation, he managed to pick the locks of his fetters and escaped from the guard. A reward of five guineas was promised to anyone who should lodge him in any of His Majesty's gaols in Great Britain. The description of the man is worth quoting:

> The said Thomas Parry is between 30 and 40 years of age, about 5ft. 6ins. high, regular set of features, fresh complexion, very black, lank or straight hair, beard of the same colour, thick set, rather broad than otherwise, and dark eyes; had on when he escaped a thickset fustian frock, greasy leather breeches and a black handkerchief round his neck; is a native of Herefordshire and lived last in the parish of Lions Hall.

I have been able to find no record of his recapture.

In all the accounts I have read of this event, I have found no mention of the motive of the attack, although what seems obvious is that these men were giving expression to a general feeling of resentment against the millers.

Place-names

The ascription of meanings to place-names is often purely speculative; my own speculations were submitted to an expert in this science, Dr. Margaret Gelling of Birmingham University, and I am grateful to her for a number of corrections and useful suggestions. A few names have been explained in the foregoing text, so they are omitted here. Some names in this list have disappeared or are unknown to be as existing at present.

Aston (O.S. 463 625): Eston in 1390. 'East tun' ('tun' early acquired the meanings 'homestead, village').

Basket Gate (O.S. 455 633): close to Oaker Wood. Could it describe a gate of wickerwork or a gate where baskets were made and sold?

Bore Fields: Bore Field in 1709. The name suggests 'boar field'.

Burlands (*cf.* map of 1709): in the bailiff's accounts of 1389–90 this occurs as 'Borlond' and in 'Burlondesdiche'. O.E. *bur land,* 'land occupied by peasants'.

Broomy Hill (O.S. 404 596); 'hill covered with broom'.

Bylets (*cf.* map of 1709); a plot near the Dayhouse meadow. There is a great house near Pembridge called Byletts (O.S. 383 583) and several examples of the name occur in Shropshire. The name appears also as Bilets. A 'bilet' is a willow-plantation. An island in the river Severn at Bridge-north, which looks as though it was formed by cutting a channel from the river to rejoin it downstream, is called the Bylet: here the channel may have been the original 'by-let'.

Caseny: the map of 1709 shows several fields with this name: Caseny Common Field, Lug Kaseny Common Field, Knackers Caseny. The name does not occur in the 1390 accounts. Dr. Gelling thinks the final element is *-ieg,* 'island'.

Cholstrey (O.S. 466 596): in Domesday Book, 'Cerlestreu'; 1709, Chorlstree ('churl's tree').

Cobnash (O.S. 450 603); Copton Ash, 1709. 'Cop Nesh' also occurs. O.E. *copp,* 'top'; Nash, aet ð aem aesce and M.E. *atten ashe,* 'rise surmounted by an ash tree'.

Croase (O.S. 444 616): now the name of a large house at the crossroads. A farm (O.S. 477 635) slightly east of Oaker Wood bears the same name. Both are perhaps variants of Welsh *croes,* 'cross'. In the first case it could refer to the crossing of the roads.

Cursney Hill (O.S. 476 593); the name is pronounced locally ka:zn. In the 19th century it was sometimes written 'Curzen'. An 1842 map gives 'Custna Hill'. As the hill was fortified by earthworks in prehistoric and Roman times, Jonathan Williams, the schoolmaster historian of 1808, finding an older form of the name to be 'Caerneveh' suggested it was derived from Brit. *caer niewe,* 'new camp' ('new' in relation to Ivington camp 5km. south of it). Dr. Gelling says that only earlier spellings would produce a satisfactory etymology for Cursney. She thinks the final element is *-ieg,* 'island'.

Fair Field: west of the church, the field on which the annual fair was held.

Fowden (O.S. 446 633): 'fow' is possibly from O.E. *fag,* 'variegated'. O.E. *denu* 'dene or valley'.

Hinton (O.S. 411 597): Henton, 1390. O.E. Hea-tun, dat. Hean-tune, 'tun situated on high ground'.

Holgate: a farm in the village. Holgete, 1390. Howgate, 1790. 'Gate in a hollow'.

Kindon: Kyndon, 1640. O.E. *'kine down'.*

Lawton (once a manor) (O.S. 446 595): Launton, 1390. This form suggests 'long tun', but Dr. Gelling thinks 'Laun' could be the genitive case of the personal name Lafa, 'lafa's tun'.

Ledicot (O.S. 415 620): Bannister suggests 'Lida's cottage', but 'Our Lady's cottage' is possible: *cf.* Lady Day, Lady Meadow and Lady Pool, the source in Shobdon Marsh of the Pinsley Brook, which flowed beneath the old Priory in Leominster before emptying itself into the Lugg. Ledicot might have belonged to a chantry. 'Ladihale' is found in 1390.

Longford: the road leaving Kingsland in the direction of Leominster. 'Ford' here looks as it if means 'causeway'.

Mardevell or Merdevall: in 1649 this was a pasture with one or two cottages adjacent to Court grove and Lyme Croft. 'Lyme-croft' occurs in the 1390 accounts. In Shrewsbury an ancient street is called Mardol and this has early spellings 'Mardevol', etc. The name is unknown in Kingsland today.

Mousenatch (O.S. 468 605): the name of a small farm which has now disappeared. It looks like an encroachment upon the common land, for it lay between Caseney Common Field and Lord's Meadow in 1709. Burland bordered it on the west. So named, perhaps, because it was a 'nibble', snatched from the common land. On a 1709 map of Lord Bateman's estate it is actually written as 'The Mouse Snatch'.

Oaker Wood or Coppice: 3 km. NNE of church. Okere, 1390.

Sodgeley (445 627): Shodgeley, 1709. The first element is not to be explained without early spellings; the second element is *leah*, 'glade'.

Street (O.S. 426 603): Strete, 'lestret' in Domesday Book. Named after the Roman road which passed through it.

The Tars or Tarrs (O.S. 442 632): the hill, 2km. NNW. of the church. 'Tar' is a form of *tor*, a Celtic or British word meaning a high rock, or pile of rocks, generally on top of a hill. The plural form may be due to the former existence of more than one pile.

Waterslades: the fields bordering the river Lugg west of Lugg bridge. O.E. *slaed*, 'valley, dell'. Waterslade occurs in 1390. The map of 1709 has 'Waterstadts'. O.E. *staep*, plural, *staeð es*: 'shore, riverbank'.

Wegnals or Wegnall: the pastures on either side of the Pinsley brook west of Cholstrey and north of Cursney hill, and where the river meanders violently, forming the 'figure of eight' (*c.* O.S. 477 595). Another Wegnall occurs on the Hindwell brook near Rodd and Presteigne in a similar location (*c.* O.S. 323 630). The first elements suggests 'wiggle' or 'wag', perhaps referring to the river's meanderings. O.E. *wagian*, with *halh*, 'river meadow'.

Weston and West Town: west-tun.

MONKLAND

Chapter Twenty

EARLY HISTORY

MONKLAND LIES NEARLY 4km. south-west of Leominster and, like the other villages in this book, derives its name from its situation in a region formerly called the Lene (of which the termination '-land' is a modification which made more sense to the Saxon conquerors of this previously Welsh or British territory). As we have seen, 'lene' or Leon implies a region of streams, and this one is well watered by many rivers of which the largest are the Arrow, Lugg and Pinsley. Monkland itself stands on the Arrow. The Metropolis of the Leon from, at latest, the Saxon conquest of *c*. 660 A.D. was Leominster, the Leon minster or monastic church. The fact that the earlier British name of this place was Llanllieni (meaning the same as Leon-minster) suggests that the town had this prominence before the coming of the Germanic Saxons; indeed, St. David's earliest biographer declares that David himself founded a monastery at Leominster.

Older names of Monkland, as found in ancient documents are Lena, Leine (in Domesday Book), Munkelen (*c*. 1180), Moneclene, Monckeslane (in Pipe Rolls), so the name means simply 'that part of the Lene which belongs to the monks'.

It would appear that the first monks who gave their name to the part of the Leon now called Monkland were those who came from the Abbey of St. Peter of Castellione at Conches in Normandy, when Ralph de Todeni gave the land to this abbey in the reign of William Rufus. Soon after the Norman Conquest, Monkland had been given to Ralph as part of his reward for his services as one of the Conqueror's standard-bearers. It is likely that de Todeni was a member of a family settled near Conches.

76

Street, the 19th-century restorer of Monkland church, states that the walls of the church date from about 1100 A.D., so the little colony of monks sent from Conches must have lost no time in getting started.

In order to make their tenure of the land more secure, between 1186 and 1199 (the period in which William de Vere was bishop of Hereford) the Benedictine monks of Conches obtained an instrument from the bishop which confirmed them in their possessions: '. . . wishing to look forward to our beloved brethren, the Abbot of St. Peter of Castellione and the monks there serving God, we grant and by our episcopal authority do confirm the Manor of Monkeslen, and the Church of the same village with the whole tithings and the rest of the profits and all things to it of right belonging, reserved a decent maintenance for the Vicar'. The document (which is a copy made by a Notary Public of the original supplied to him in 1433 by Robert le Ryve, a monk and priest of Conches), gives a list of the properties belonging to the community in Monkland.

The religious house thus established was always very small, though the property was not inconsiderable. Much of the income from this would have gone to the mother-house at Conches. The community of two or three Black Benedictine monks was a cell of Conches, and was linked to another cell at Wootton Wawen in Warwickshire which had only two to four monks. These 'cells' were scarcely monasteries, for the few monks who inhabited them could not have lived the regular life of prayer and worship in anything like the fullness which is possible within a large community. The resident monks were sent by the mother-house to exploit a distant estate and forward some of its revenues to head-quarters. Dom David Knowles, the great historian of medieval monasteries, says they were never a source of strength and soon came to be used as refuges for the unemployed, or places of exile for *mauvais sujets*.

The tenure of Monkland, an 'alien priory', was precarious. In common with other houses of its class, it was liable to be seized by the Crown whenever war broke out between England and France. With the larger neighbouring Priory

of Leominster (which was a cell of Reading Abbey) it often
suffered from the violence of the border feuds. In spite
of these embarrassments, the monks improved their land
and in about 1220 they were able to build the church tower;
c. 1270 they inserted new windows.

In 1399, during the wars with France, it was handed
over by Richard II to the Carthusian monks of Coventry,
who also received its sister cell of Wootton Wawen. It appears
that it was later returned to the Abbey of Conches, but the
mother-house could have enjoyed its revenues for only a
short time because all the alien priories were finally suppressed by the parliament held at Leicester in 1414.

In 1415 Henry V made a grant of the cell of Monkland and
all its properties to Sir Rowland Lenthall, who had distinguished himself at the battle of Agincourt. Sir Rowland is
said to have enriched himself greatly by the ransoms he was able
to exact for the prisoners he had taken in the battle. With this
wealth, according to Leland, he was able to begin the building
of Hampton Court on another of his Herefordshire properties.

While Monkland was the property of the Lenthalls the
church does not appear to have been improved or restored.
They had it for only 50 years, for, resumed by the Crown, it
was granted in 1475 to the Dean and Canons of Windsor, whose
property it remained until 1831. Then, says the Rev. C. J.
Robinson, writing in 1872, 'it was exchanged with W. Preece
of Leominster, whose son sold it in 1835 to George Bengough
of The Ridge, Gloucestershire, whose son now enjoys it'.

As at Leominster the monastery was distinct from the
parish church which had its own rector or vicar, though
the Abbey of Conches, or later, the Lenthalls and the Dean
and Canons of Windsor, had the right to present him.

Nothing is really known of the influence of the monks
of Conches upon local agriculture. The fact that Conches
is the heart of the French apple-growing district has been
noticed, and some writers have thought that the monks sent
to Monkland did something to improve the apple, for which
Herefordshire later became so famous. As no one knows
how the apple as a palatable fruit was introduced into the
shire, the theory is tenable.

Chapter Twenty-One

THE MANOR AND ITS ORGANISATION

THE MANOR OF MONKLAND is co-extensive with the parish. Its lords from Norman times until 1831, apart from the short period 1414–1474, were ecclesiastical, and, like lay lords, they obtained their income from the rents, fines and heriots paid by their tenants. A lay lord held his land on the understanding that he rendered military services when called upon. His interest, therefore, was to secure a succession of vassals to follow him to war. Over the progeny of his tenants he exercised the authority of a guardian, using his influence in such a way as to inure the young men to hardship and to train them in the arts of a soldier, for to him such attainments were more important than excellence in the cultivation of the soil. For these reasons the lay lord generally permitted the tenants a continuous property in the soil. They possessed an inheritance, though on the death of a tenant the lord took the best beast (formerly the war-horse) and the best chattel (formerly the arms) as a 'heriot' or fine. In time certain incidents followed from this, including guardianship, when the estate was held in copyhold as a dower to a wife after her husband's death. For this, large payments were demanded as fines on the tenant's death or on his retiring from the tenancy.

In manors like Monkland held by ecclesiastical proprietors, a different kind of tenure was usual, termed 'copyhold for lives'. The manor was usually leased and the person who held it was styled the Lord Rector or Lord Farmer, and the courts were held in his name. The number of lives permitted to be named in this class of manor varied. In many, as in Monkland, it was three. The tenant had to pay an annual 'quit

79

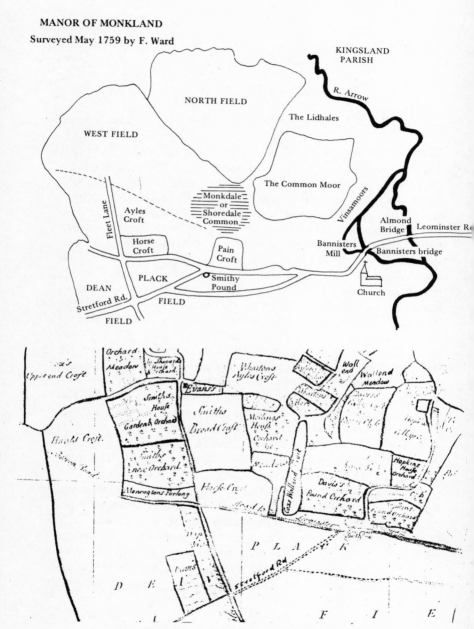

MANOR OF MONKLAND

Surveyed May 1759 by F. Ward

The Manor of Monkland after Enclosure

rent'. He had the liberty to add a new life on the falling in of any of the three lives, on condition of paying the appropriate fine, which never exceeded two years' rent.

Imperfect as this type of tenure appears, it will be seen to be consistent with the interests of ecclesiastical lords: they neither rendered nor required military services. They sought a reasonable return in rent and fines, and the cultivation of the soil. Custom and practice in Monkland tend to confirm this assertion, for the heriot was not the best beast or chattel; it was a quarter of the quit rent only. The lords granted leave to each newly-accepted tenant to grant a lease for a considerable term, and thus was avoided the obvious difficulty of occupying under a tenure so uncertain in its determination. Yet the fact that capital was invested in the soil and a high state of cultivation had been attained must be attributed to a confidence engendered by usage and just dealings in the past.

Most of the tenants of the manor of Monkland were copyholders, and in 1760 these numbered forty-two. In addition there were 15 freeholders. The free tenants held their land under the usual terms, fealty, suit of court and an annual rent. In 1722, 10 of these voted in the county election. Eleven voted in 1802 and 1818.

As in most English manors before the Enclosure movement of the late 18th and early 19th centuries, the manor of Monkland was farmed on the open-field system. Tenants cultivated acre strips in the common fields, all growing the same crop in each field. The number of strips held varied from tenant to tenant. Ploughing, sowing and reaping had to be done by everyone at the same times, which were agreed upon at the manorial court. A good deal of co-operation was needed to make the system work smoothly. All tenants had the right to pasture animals in the common field or moor, and the number of beasts each tenant could put on the common was regulated by the manorial court, to whose decisions all tenants were subject. The great open fields are shown on the accompanying map: the North field, the West Field, the Plack or Pleck field, and Dean field. The map shows that in 1759 there were also a number of fields owned or leased. These were perhaps the plots, some of which had been joined, of earlier tenants; for medieval peasants, besides the strips in the common open fields, had fair-sized plots on which their houses stood. These were cultivated for herbs and vegetables and sustained poultry and a few pigs.

The fact that open-field cultivation appears to have lasted much longer in Monkland than in Herefordshire as a whole could possible result from its being ecclesiastical property until 1831.

As has been mentioned, the activities of the farming community were regulated by a court of record known as the court baron or court leet, presided over by the lord or his steward. The court also heard complaints of unsocial behaviour, levied fines and issued orders on fixed annual dates; thus it ordered that gates of the common be hung and fences made by 29 September. Another order required the same to be done for the Lent fields by 10 February; cattle were to be removed from the moor by 15 November, and a penalty was laid upon those who kept any kind of cattle or any living thing in the corn or Lent fields before the last sheaf or 'cock' was carried away. Anyone keeping more than two sheep an acre on the common field was also liable to a fine.

In Monkland, the common meadows were called the Moors and the Fleets. The latter were sometimes distinguished as the Upper, Middle or Lower Fleets, or as the Mowing Fleets, or the Cow Fleets.

Transference of land was executed before a special court baron. The land which had been held as copyhold was surrendered to the steward as representing the lord of the manor. Thus: 'John Rogers of Leominster, Shoemaker, and Charles Rogers, Druggist, customary Tenants of the Manor . . . surrendered to the Lords by the hands of their Steward and by *the Rod according to the Custom* all that dwelling house . . . etc., known by the name of the "Travellers Arms" but now called "The Red Lion".' The steward then conveyed the land to its new tenant by a symbolic delivery.

THE COMMON MOOR

William Preece, a solicitor of Leominster, acquired the Manor of Monkland from the Dean and Canons of Windsor by exchanging it for a freehold estate of 157 acres of annual value of £160, in the parish Ullingswick. This William Preece was the son of a William Preece of Yatton, Aymestrey, who owned a paper-mill there (this mill, later turned over to corn milling, was in use until the 1950s).

Preece's tenure of the Manor of Monkland was brief. It was settled upon him by an Act of 1831, but he sold it in 1835 to George Bengough of Gloucestershire. Since then it has remained in the possession of the Bengoughs or their trustees.

Chapter Twenty-Two

CHANGES IN THE MODE OF LAND TENURE

THOUGH THE Enclosure Acts were not applied to the Manor of Monkland, other Acts were passed in the 19th century to end copyhold and customary tenure. These Acts enabled the tenants, for a sum of money, to free themselves from manorial demands once and for all. To quote the Act of 1852: the property is 'to be holden as freehold henceforth and for ever discharged from all fines, heriots, reliefs, quit rents and all other incidents whatsoever of copyhold or customary tenure'.

Gradually people availed themselves of the new rights. In 1890 an award of enfranchisement was made by the Board of Agriculture to Thomas and Michael Beard of Leominster for Board property scattered about the Manor of Monkland, for which they paid £99 15s. 0d. Others followed.

A further Act of 1894 enabled copyhold (subject to the consent of the Board of Agriculture) to be converted into freehold. By the Law of Property Act of 1922, all copyhold land was enfranchised. Copyhold tenure was abolished, together with customary freehold tenure.

Chapter Twenty-Three

THE PARISH OFFICERS AND THEIR WORK

THE HISTORIAN of Monkland is fortunate in having at his disposal two leather-bound Parish Books which record the election of parish officers at annual vestry meetings, their decisions from time to time, and their work and expenditure. The first of the two books records transactions from 1730 until 1817; the second, from 1817 until the present day, for it is still in use. Thus we have a continuous record of the work of churchwardens, overseers of the poor, and overseers of highways, or waywardens, for 244 years, or as long as these officials existed from 1730 onwards. Book I opens with the Articles of Agreement signed by representatives of the inhabitants of Monkland.

........at a Visitation, when the new Churchwardens and the two Sidesmen are sworn, they shall not on the Parish Charge, Amount to and Expend upwards of the sum of Ten Shillings.

.......upon Easter Monday the old officers are to make a due and just return of Two Able and Sufficient men to the Parish to Succeed them in the ensuing year.

.......the Officers of a Churchwarden Collector of his May Taxes Both Land and Litemonies, and likewise the Overseer of the Poor and Likewise the next year Following the same Two Officers shall Serve the office of a Surveyor for the year ensuing.

.......they must not cause to be done anything more than what's their Office . . . without a just allowance from the inhabitants.

........They may be paid 2 shillings for drawing up the Parish accounts.

.......At monthly meetings no more than 1 shilling to be expended.

.......The minister to be given 1 shilling for drawing out the transcript. [The copy of the church register demanded each year by the bishop.]

86

. . . . . . .In Case of disagreements among the Inhabitants about things not expressed in the Articles, then the Major Voice of any Vestry shall give in according to their Judgements.

The Articles are signed by the officers, William Griffiths and Richard Sheward. The book gives lists of petty constables (1732–1793), surveyors of highways (1731–1791), and overseers of the poor.

The Poor Law Act of 1601 made each parish responsible for the care of its own poor. To finance this service, parishes were expected to levy a rate, called in Monkland a 'lewn' or loan, of so much in the pound, upon occupiers of land or property. To administer this fund, the parishioners nominated overseers of the poor, who received their appointments from the Justices of the Peace. Besides the overseers of the poor, the meeting of parishioners (the vestry) also appointed a surveyor or overseer of highways, or waywarden, whose work was to keep the parish roads in good order. He, too, had funds at his disposal. Sometimes the two functions of overseer of the poor and waywarden were combined.

The overseers made regular weekly payments to the impotent poor—the aged, the sick and young children, who needed support. At first these people lived in their own cottages, for which the rent was sometimes paid. The bills of doctors and midwives attending them were paid, and food, clothing and coal were provided when necessary. Funeral expenses were found when poor parishioners died. The disbursements of the overseers were recorded in the Parish Book and make interesting reading. The multifarious activities of the overseers surprise one, and it is not uncommon to find them handing over their arduous task to a paid official from time to time. They selected the men to serve in the militia, and took the census. They also saw to the maintenance of the stocks, the pound, gates, and so on.

In October 1761 we find this entry which marks the introduction of a workhouse in Monkland (the Workhouse Act of 1722 had given leave to parishes to provide such houses for the poor, and people declining to enter them could be refused relief):

'An Agreement between the Inhabitants and John Preece, i.e. the said John Preece shall take, keep, provide for and maintain the poor of the said Parish of Monkland in a good proper and sufficient manner and Orders as is customary in Common Workhouses, and that, the said Inhabitants shall pay the said John Preece the sum of £12 a year, And also that the said John Preece shall have one-third part of the said £12 in hand.' Fourteen inhabitants signed.

John Preece appears to have found the burden too great for him, or his remuneration too little for the work he did, for the next year the parishioners made an agreement with one Thomas Leech:

'1762   Agreement made with Thomas Leech to take, keep, Nourish and Maintain in Sickness, Health or otherwise the Poor. The inhabitants to pay him £13 for one year; one pound now in hand and the like sum the 1st of every month ensuing. He must deliver up to the overseers all the goods he shall receive with the Poor Person or Persons lodged under his care. At the end of the year he must "cloath and aray the said poor people" as well as they were clothed when he received them. Parish to pay for any funerals. Leech is to allow inhabitants to visit at any time unmolested to inspect the conduct and behaviour of himself towards the poor people in his care.' The agreement was signed by Thomas Leech and 10 inhabitants.

A similar agreement was made in 1764 with one Thomas King of Broxwood, who had more staying power. He was paid £14 a year until 1768 when John Thomas took on the management of the workhouse. In 1787 we find the following entry' 'To James Williams for Half a Years Rent of the Workhouse 17s. 6d.'. The workhouse was kept for years at this rent, but on 28 May 1795 it was agreed by the vestry to pay James East £30 to maintain the poor of the parish for one year in sufficient 'Diet, Cloathing and Lodging'. He was at liberty 'to employ (if he chuses it) such of the Poor as are able in such Work and Services as may tend to his own best Advantage'.

There is no explanation as to why his payment the next year is so greatly reduced:

	£	s.	d.
1796 To James East in all for the Workhouse ..	17	10	0
To do. do. for his trouble	2	6	4
and the overseers for 1797 record			
James East for Hussey, Powell, Lyming ..	1	0	0

The workhouse seems to have been given up and the practice of relieving the poor in their own homes to have been resumed. In 1821, however, at a vestry meeting, a house was hired to lodge poor people: '. . . I agree on consent to let Thomas Lewis House to the Parish *Offiseers* for the use of the Paupers of the said Parish at the yearly rent of two Pounds ten shillings for the Tenure of five years, the Parish to keep the House in Tenantable repair. As Witness Wm Perry juner'.

In 1813 the parish vestry decided to relieve the overseers of their obligations to the poor by deputing their work to a paid man:

'. . . we whose names are hear and subscribed being Inhabitants of the Parish of Monkland Doth on this Eighth Day of May 1813 we jointly agree, grant and consent that Michael Beard shall act as Standing Officer for the space of Seven Years, he continew as long in the Parish.

'First to give him four pounds, four shillings a year and each Overseer, when they are appointed, to give him 10s. 6d. to acknowledge the Turn of such Person . . .

'Secondly that he shall keep the Accounts Regurly Past, and the Loans made and Sig^nd by the Majestrates at his own Expence. All other Jurneys he shall be Paid for, and Reasonable Expenses aloud by the Parish.

'Witness   Geo. Pigot, John Smith, John Rogers.'

The first page of Book II (purchased in February 1817 for 11s. 0d.) lists, 'The Lewns granted to Michael Beard as Acting Overseer for Thos and Saml Parker:

' 4 April 1816 — a shilling rate	£53	4	6
18 July 1816 — a sixpenny rate	£26	12	6
12 Dec. 1816 — a shilling rate	£53	4	6
11 Jan. 1817 — a fourpenny rate ..	£17	8	2 '

In the year 25 March 1816 - 25 March 1817, Mr. Beard
had to make weekly payments to six poor people, ranging
from 1s. 6d. to 4s. 0d. a week. Three other people received
regular weekly doles of 2s.–3s. for 16 to 27 weeks. To obtain
some idea of the value of these sums, it is as well to know
that a farm-labourer of this period was paid 7s.–8s. a week
with which to support himself and his family. The recipients
of these doles were at this time living in their own homes.
When necessary the overseer made additional payments. One
poor person, Charlotte Humphreys, was maintained at 9d.
a week in the home of Elizabeth Powell. Charlotte twice
received extra pay 'by consent'. Charlotte appears to have
been more than usually fortunate, for we find the following
entries:

Sept. 16	Journey to the Infirmary with Charlotte	12s.	0d.
Nov. 10	Charlotte's lodging at Pughs ..	2s.	0d.
Feb. 1817	Bill for Charlotte's board at infirmary	10s.	0d.
5 May 1817	Charlotte to buy Salt Petre ..	1s.	0d.
	Flannel for Charlotte		6d.

One lady whose name occurs more frequently than others
in the account of the overseers is Jane Baylis. Indeed, with
the information one can glean from the church registers to
supplement the overseers' record, her life history is better
documented than that of most of her contemporaries.

Jane, the daughter of Richard and Ann Baylis, was baptised on 11 June 1769. She had three brothers. Her parents
were poor, her father being a farm labourer. In 1782 when
she was 13 and her brother William 10, the overseer paid
for their apprenticeship to different masters. The overseers'
account will tell the story of Jane's life:

		£	s.	d.
1782	To Mr. Jones with Jane Baylis, his apprentice		10	0
1797	Jane Baylis		1	0
1802	Shirt for Lyke & Apron for Jane Baylis		5	6
	Relieved Jane Baylis		3	6
	Paid Thos. Smith for a pair of shoes for Jane Baylis		5	6

		£	s.	d.
1802	Relieve Jane Baylis when ill		5	0
1813–	Jane Baylis 53 weeks at 2s. 6d.	6	12	6
1815	Journey to Weobley with Jane Baylis ..		2	6
	[presumably to the Petty Sessions, accused of theft]			
	Paid to Galor for Jane Baylis while in prison		10	6
	Paid Jane Baylis for Cloth and Mending Parish Sheets		3	6
	Journey to Leominster for Jane Baylis not to have her pay rose		2	6
	Journey to Leominster concerning J. Baylis		2	6
1815– 16	Jane Baylis. 27 weeks at 2s. 6d.) 20 weeks at 2s. 6d.)	5	7	6
1816	Nov. 12. Pd Jane Baylis to Bring her Clos from Pawn		5	0
1816– 1817	Jane Baylis 52 weeks at 3s. 0d. .. .. Paid J. Baylis extra 1s. 0d.	7	16	0
1816	Dec 12. Jane Baylis to bring her clothes out of pawn		5	0
1817	10th May. Jane Baylis to go to London ..	1	10	0
	6th July. 2 cwt coal for Jane Baylis ..		3	0
1819	24 Feb. Jane Baylis expenses going to London	1	5	0
1825	15 Jan. Coffin and Shroud for Jane Baylis	1	5	0

She died at the age of fifty-six.

The parish was always anxious to avoid the burden of extra responsibilities and tried therefore to obtain money from the father of an illegitimate child. We find this entry for 7 May 1762:

'Thos Evans the Elder and Thos Evans the Younger both of this parish and Thos Worthington of Kington gave bond for fifty pounds to indemnifie the Parish for a Bastard child begotten on the Body of Ann Gwillim by the said Thos. Evans. the Younger wch bond is in the hands of Thos. Morris Overseer of the Poor of this Parish. N.B. The said child is since Dead and the Bond is gave up.'

Later: '1781. Going with the Constable to apprehend the Fellow on whom Ann Powles swore her child 2s. 6d.'

'1782. N.B. The above mentioned John Jones (the one to whom Jane Baylis was apprenticed) was one, who, having served his apprenticeship in this Parish and thereby gaining a Settlement, came with his wife and Children to seek for Relief and were accordingly relieved, but it was afterwards proved that the said Hannah was not his lawful wife, being married to him whiles he had a former wife living, and consequently the children were illegitimate. Whereupon, after a Lawsuit with the Parish of Bromyard, the Parish to which the woman belonged, she and her children were sent to their respective parishes, and the expenses of their Maintenance during their stay were recovered of the said Parish of Bromyard, by the lawsuit above mentioned.'

'1830.   22 Jan.   Taking Mary Ann Hughes to Lemster to swear to her bastard child.   2s. 6d.'.

Military Service

The overseers were also concerned with the selection of men to serve in the militia. Each shire was required to furnish its quota of men for the defence of the nation. These men were expected to undergo a certain number of days' training each year. As a rule the militia was raised by voluntary recruitment, but, if this failed, a levy by ballot could be made upon all men in the locality between the ages of 18 and 50, though many classes were exempted. The men of Monkland do not seem always to have been willing:

'Robert Jones for the Upper End, Francis Jones for the Pleck appointed 17th Oct. 1787 to serve instead of Mr. Wharton who had been first appointed, but ballotted afterwards to serve in the Militia.'

During the French wars, 1808–1812, a series of local Militia Acts were passed to create a new compulsory 'home guard', consisting of men between eighteen and thirty. In April 1804 we read of the overseers:

'Paid James Moor who was Ballotted for the Army of Reserve for this Parish.   £6.0.0.'

'Paid William Jones being Ballotted for the Old Militia. £5.0.0.'.

In 1815: 'Paid for two substitutes for the 2nd Battalion Militia.   £2.0.0'.

'Paid Major Ross to procure ditto   5s. 0d.'.
In 1817: 'Journey to Kington with Militia List   7s. 0d.'.

Pest Control

In July 1792 the parish vestry agreed that the expenses of catching and destroying birds should be paid out of poor loan. Later, rats appear to have been included:

		£	s.	d.
1794	To the Ratcatcher	1	5	11
1817	Wm. Lloyd for catching Birds		5	6
1830	Paid Edward Greenhouse for catching birds in the Parish. 18 doz.		13	6
1836	Pd. Ed. Greenhouse for catching 40 doz. birds at 5d. a doz.		16	8

Care of the Pound, the Stocks, Gates, Bridges

The overseers were empowered by the vestry to expend sums on the maintenance of various public facilities. In fact they could be fined by the court leet if they did not keep the stocks, the pound, gates, and so on, in proper order. Here are some of their disbursements for these purposes:

		£	s.	d.
1738	To Mr Smith for Rent for the Pound ..		11	3
1739	for the Garden at the Pound..		1	0
	for keeping Palmer's gate		1	6
	pd Mr Smyth half a years rent for the Pound house		11	3
	pd Alexander Colcomb for mending the Stocks		1	8
1758	For the Moor Gate		16	6
	Pd George Jones for mending the Stocks		1	3
1819	Watkins for raising stone for the Pound 11s.) Thos. Smith ,, ,, ,, ,, ,, 12s.)	1	3	0
	Pd S. Parker his Bill for hauling stone to Pound and 2 Posts	1	19	11
	for Timber to make Pound Gate		3	0
	Pd Mr. Weyman for 82 Bushall Lime at 10d. .. .. £3.8.4) Preece & Son for raising Stones £2.7.0)	5	15	0

The care of the bridges was part of the work of the surveyor or overseer of highways.

			£	s.	d.
1743	for pitching Causeways & Mending Bridges			4	6
	Seven load stone			3	6
1804	Repairing Rails at Hay's Bridge			13	10

In 1817 a Mr. Samuel Peploe, presumably a county official, had demanded that the parish officers should impose a collection of 2s. 6d. in the pound to pay for repairs to the roads in the parish. In reply they wrote begging him not to enforce this expense on the poor farmers. They solemnly understook to keep the highways in good order, adding 'We are not conscious of any part of the Turnpike Road in our Parish being out of order'. Nevertheless, in the three years ending in April 1821 the Surveyor of the Highways, Mr. John Weyman, had to expend a good deal of money:

		£	s.	d.
14 Jan. 1819	Paid Watkins for raising 50 ... gravel ..	2	1	8
Feb. 1820	Paid for Stone for the Bridge Building at Arrow Green	4	18	0
Mar. 1820	Pd for 100 ... Gravel	4	3	4
	Pd for forming Arrow Green Road, 530 yards at 5d. a yard	11	0	10
	One day's work		1	6
	Mr Evans for 3000 Brick for the Bridge	5	0	0
	Stone for the Bridge	5	0	0
	Baskerville's fees		5	0
	110 Bushall Lime	4	1	8
	Mr. Gethen's Bill for making the bridge	5	14	1
	New Wheelbarrow		16	0
1822 April	Smith for work in the Road. 14 days		11	8
June	Smith for work on Road. 36 Perch at 1s.	1	16	0
July	Magnage [Magness] for work in the Road	1	11	1
	Fletcher's Bill for Hammers.		6	1
Oct.	Paid Watkins for raising stone	4	3	4
Dec.	Oliver for breaking 5 Ton of Stone at 10d		4	2
1829 —	John Evans 4 days work on Road ..		4	6
	Sam Boddy. 8 days work on common Bridge		8	0
	Plates and Nails for Flit Gate.. ..		0	10½

The Churchwardens' Accounts

The responsibility of this office are well illustrated by the lists of his disbursements.

1758	£	s.	d.
To the Visitation at Hereford		8	6
Bread and Wine at Christmas, Easter and Whitsuntide. 3s. 11d. each time		15	8
Washing and mending the 'Surpless'..		3	6
Cleaning the Plate		1	6
Prayer for a Fast		1	6
Allowed Mr Wharton for the Church	1	16	7

The one regular item missed out here is payment for the transcript of the church register which had to be made out annually and sent to the bishop (this will be seen in later accounts). The churchwardens had to see to the repair and decoration of the church. In 1774 the churchwarden had difficulties with the painter:

	£	s.	d.
To Tanner for his dirty colours		5	0
To ditto to leave off daubing the Church		1	0
To John Neale Painter for ornamenting the Church..	3	0	0
To a folio Church Common Prayer		17	0
2nd payment to Neale the Painter		13	6

1817–1818 Edward Morris, Churchwarden	£	s.	d.
Bread and Wine for the Church		4	6
Wm Lloyd for benches		6	0
Pd for Transcripts		2	6
Joseph Magnage [Magness] Clerk	2	8	0
for washing the surplice..		3	0
Paid Mr Lloyd for work done to the church.. ..		6	10
Richard Hurly for repairing the do.	1	4	0
Paid Samuel Body for work done do.		5	0
Paid at the Visitation	2	2	0
two hundred nailes for the Bells		1	4
board, 10½d, hoope 1s, for the Bells		1	10½
Wm Hay for repering the wall round the Churchyard		5	0

Mr. John Weyman, churchwarden, listed his disbursements over the three years ending April 1826:

	£	s.	d.
Paid Rowden Smith for Mason's work	4	13	2
Parish Clerk's fees for 3 years	6	6	0
Three years at the Visitation	3	3	0
Fees for 3 years with the Presentments		13	0
Bread and Wine for the Sacrament for 3 years..	2	5	0
Magnane for cleaning the Church		7	6
Making matts for the Church		19	0
Straw for making matts		16	0
Glazier's Bill		12	7
3 Fees for altering the form of Prayer at 4s. 6d. each		13	6

The churchwardens seem to have had to renew bell ropes
(three for £1 1s. d. in 1828) often, for the ringers, supplied
with ale at parish expense, 'rang with a will', especially on
5 November each year. The churchwarden had to supply
broom and brush for the cleaner (3s. 10d.) and parchment
for the transcripts (3s. 0d.).

Miscellaneous Gleanings from the Overseers' Accounts

The overseers paid for the medical care of the necessitous
poor. Some of the items are surprising, others amusing, e.g.:
'1842 Curing Pulley of the Itch 8d.'.

In 1785 the overseer had brought ointment for the cure
of the itch for 6d., so the complaint appears to have been
prevalent. Women occasionally gave birth to children when on
poor relief. The following entries for 1739 are remarkably
detailed:

	£	s.	d.
for flanin for Whittles		2	8
for fetching the Midwife at midnight		2	8
paid the Midwife		3	0
for taking her whome		2	8
for drink and other nesicaris at her Labour ..		2	8
Pd Kate Whitby for sustinance for her		1	0
aloud Kate for House room and nursing 6 weeks		12	0
pd Samuel Whitby for baring the Childe			8
for Bread and Sugar in her weakness			8

Doctor's bills must have worried the overseers considerably:

1819 5 Feb. Allowed Mr Hull to pay doctor's
      bill for C(harlotte) Humphreys..   ..   2   0   0

1824 The Old Overseers had a Surgeon's Bill of near Twenty
      Pounds to pay for a Casualty of a Man being run over
      by a Waggon which was not as yet collected from the
      Inhabitants.

The overseers occasionally had to pay postage on letters.
Before Rowland Hill's introduction of the Penny Post in
1840, the cost of a letter varied with the distance it travelled;
we find these entries in the Parish Book:

1817 Postage of a Letter from Eliz. Taylor
      from Worcester   ..   ..   7d.
1818 Postage of a letter to the Overseers   ..   9d.
1822 Postage of a Letter to the parish from
      London   ..   ..   10d.
      [The recipient paid the postage]
1831 Postage of 2 letters   ..   ..   8d.
      Postage of a letter   ..   ..   1s. 0d.

Prices

1786 Pair of Shoes   ..   ..   5s. 0d.
      2 Shirts ..   ..   7s. 0d.
      Frock [Smock] ..   ..   4s. 0d.
      Waistcoat ..   ..   5s. 0d.
1817 A Shift   ..   ..   2s. 0d.
      Sheets [presumably a pair]   ..   ..   ..   6s. 0d.
1823 Blanket   ..   ..   3s. 0d.
1831 A Pin-before [pinafore]   ..   ..   ..   1s. 0d.
1842 Hat and a pair of stockings   ..   ..   .. 2s. 0d.
      Pair of stockings   ..   ..   9d.
      Shirt   ..   ..   1s. 11d.
      Frock   ..   ..   2s. 10d.
      Mending shoes   ..   ..   2d.

People capable of work were employed if possible at the
Poor House, and materials had to be supplied by the overseers. Poor people appear to have been paid for their work
as follows:

1818 Herds for Mrs Cooke and Spinning   ..   15s. 0d.
      ['Herds' are the coarser parts of flax or
         hemp]
1819 Mending a Parish Spinning-Wheel ..   ..   6d.

1823	E. Pugh for whitening 13lbs. of Yarn..	..	2s. 2d.
	Paid for weving the 13lbs. of Yarn..	..	3s. 3d.
1836	Paid Mary Lloyd for Spinning	.. ..	10d.
	Pd. for ½ stone of Flax	.. .. ..	5s. 0d.
	pd for Making 2 shirts for . Evans..	..	1s. 0d.

The Poor House was supplied in 1821 by a Mr. Rogers with:

7 thrave boltings at	..	..	..	..	..	£2 9s. 0d.
and 1½ thrave more at ..	..	..	..	..		10s. 6d.

'Boltings' was sifted, or 'bolted' meal or corn, and a 'thrave' a measure of 24–28 sheaves.

Census

In 1811 the overseer, Mrs. Margaret Clarke, was paid 15s. 'for taking an Acc^t. of the Population of the Parish'. The overseer of 1821 charged the parish only 5s. 0d. for 'Taking the Population of Monkland', which totalled one hundred and eighty-seven.

Over the period 1816 to 1836, the last year in which outdoor relief was distributed to the parish poor, the average number of weekly recipients was eight. The number reached a maximum of 13 in 1824.

With the passing of the Poor Law Amendment Act in 1834, parishes were for economy obliged to combine in unions sharing a common workhouse. Each parish had to defray the expenses of maintaining its own poor there, and each union was to be managed by boards of Guardians elected by parish ratepayers.

Outdoor relief was practically discontinued. All able-bodied poor people were obliged to go to the workhouse (Leominster for Monkland) if they needed relief, and harsh conditions were deliberately designed to deter the poor from being supported by the parish. The fairly kindly system illustrated in these pages had come to an end.

Chapter Twenty-Four

CHARITIES

ALTHOUGH THE POPULATION of this village was always small and no wealthy landowners lived within its confines, it was not without some people who felt it incumbent upon them to provide for the poor and needy of the parish.

'Many years ago', to quote the Charity Commissioners' report of 1838, a now unknown benefactor left '10 shillings a year arising out of lands called the "Poor Acre"'. On the Tithe Map of 1841 this is shown as part of the Bunhales ('Bunhall' in the Charity Commissioners' report) on the northern boundary of the parish touching upon the River Arrow. It is obvious that the land which yielded 10s. per annum at the time of the bequest must have yielded much more as time went on, but the charity continued to receive 10s. of the currency—ever diminishing in value. Had our ancestors possessed our experience of the instability of the value of money, they would have made better provision for the future.

Another unknown donor gave a sum charged on the Pleck Estate which the returns of 1786 state was 5s. a year as rent of land. The proprietor in 1838, Mr. William Preece, was paying 3s. a year, a sum which was distributed with the Marlowe Charity.

Miss Mary Marlowe, the daughter of a rich London jeweller, lived for some time at Townsend House, Leominster. A devout Baptist, she generously endowed the Baptist chapel in that town. In 1773 she founded a number of charities in some of the neighbouring villages, and both Monkland and Eardisland were endowed with an income of 13s. 10d. a year to relieve their poor. This sum is still received from the trustees.

99

In his will of 1802 Henry Newton, gent., gave £100 in trust to the minister and churchwardens of Monkland. It was to be placed out at five per cent. and the interest was to be divided into equal portions and 'distributed to the poor of the parish in good bread every Sunday throughout the year and every year for ever'. Alas! for good intentions! By 1838 this bequest was yielding only £3 12s. 6d. per annum, and was already too small to give weekly relief to the poor. At that date bread was purchased and distributed on six or seven Sundays in the middle of winter 'to about 20 of the poorest individuals attending the service'. The donor had stipulated that the recipients should be in attendance at the parish church at the time of distribution. This Newton Bread Charity was still operating between 1914 and 1918, for at that time bread was distributed on the Sundays of Lent. The bills of the supplier, Richard Patrick of Dilwyn, are preserved in the vestry chest. The amount spent and the price of bread (presumably two-pound loaves) for Lent 1913 is revealed as '7 weeks bread. 18 loaves per week at 5d. —£2. 12s. 6d.'.

In 1924 Miss Louise Mary Sharp of Home Lodge, No. 3 Thurlow Park Road, Dulwich, who had relations (the Beards) in Monkland, a village for which she developed a great affection, left £100 to be invested in Consols, the interest from which was to be used to purchase coals for the poor of Monkland at Christmas annually. She wished the bequest to be known as 'The John Bradbeer Hemmings Trust', presumably in memory of her uncle, Mr. Hemming, who was a London bank manager, and who, like her, was a frequent visitor to Monkland. Miss Sharp died in 1928 while staying with Mr. and Mrs. William Cave at Wall End farm.

This charity still exists, though the quantity of coal it buys has diminished greatly. In 1961 the fund purchased 21 cwts of coal at 8s. 7d. per cwt.

Chapter Twenty-Five

OCCUPATIONS OF THE INHABITANTS

MONKLAND is, and always was, a village of people dependent for their life upon the land. Apart from a few essential tradesmen—the innkeepers, the blacksmith, the wheelwright, the miller, and the clergyman, the inhabitants were all engaged in farming operations. Sometimes two trades were undertaken by one man. Thus, in 1876, the landlord of the *New* inn, William Price, continued to ply his former trade of blacksmith; in 1905 Thomas Davis, proprietor of the *Red Lion*, was also the wheelwright. In 1900 'miller' had disappeared from the list of trades, but a bootmaker in the person of James Bond had made up the number. In that year one Francis Smith was both blacksmith and wheelwright.

In about 1760, of the farmers 15 were freeholders and 42 copyholders. As the total population at that time was about a hundred and eighty, the rest would have been members of their families, servants, and farm-labourers working for the others. At that time the farm-labourers received about seven shillings a week, with which, while in health, they and their families just managed to stay alive. These were 'the poor' for whom the charity bread and the occasional doles were a godsend.

Sir Henry Williams Baker kept up the tradition of Christian concern for poorer people by an annual dole of bags of grain on St. Thomas's Day (21 December). The grain was distributed after the service in the church, at which his hymn, 'Praise, O praise our God and King', was always sung. If the weather was cold and inclement, the poor recipients were afterwards invited up to Horkesley House, where they were served with bowls of hot soup prepared by Miss Jessy Baker, his sister.

Before the abandonment of the open-field system of cultivation, in which the basic cereals were grown by all the strip cultivators, there was little scope for specialisation in farming. Apple orchards and hopyards were already a feature of the area, but with the consolidation of the strips to form large holdings enclosed by hedges or fences, a number of farmers began to concentrate on the breeding of pedigree herds of Hereford cattle. Chief among these were members of the Cave family, who first appear in the church records in 1843, when Elizabeth Ann Cave was baptised on 20 August. The Caves had migrated from Rowden Abbey, near Bromyard, and have been prominent in the neighbourhood ever since. Mrs. Dorothy Speakman of Stagbatch House was born a Cave at Wall End farm in 1899, and having lived in the vicinity all her life, has been of great help to the author in his pursuit of information about Monkland.

Mrs. Dorothy Speakman's Recollections of Monkland

Mrs. Speakman is the daughter of William Henry Browne Cave, who, like her, was born at Wall End farm. She remembers several farms existing in her childhood: Manor Farm, Wall End, Little Wall End, Upper Wall End (the farmhouse was burnt down in 1905), and Next End Farms. Her father grew hops and fruit and had a pedigree herd of Herefords. In the early years of this century the Moody sisters, who lived at Horkesley House, were prominent parishioners; they were ardent church workers, benevolent to everyone in the village, and when they died the parish declined.

Mrs. Speakman also remembers that until the first World War the church choir was of a high standard, and that the school, which was efficient, always had two teachers, and from thirty to fifty pupils.

Chapter Twenty-Six

MONKLAND INNS

THE FIRST INN of which I found a record was *The Seven Stars,* at which the court leet met in 1758. The building still exists, being one of the oldest in the village; it is the cruck house known today as Church Cottage, just a little west of the bridge, near the church.

In 1868 the court met at the *New* inn, now a beautiful dwelling-house called 'The Beeches', to the left of the old road to Dilwyn, just before it re-enters the new main road. This inn had very spacious rooms in the 18th-century block which faces the road. The older, once timber-framed part of the house is at the rear. In it there is still evidence of a great fireplace with inglenooks and an end-wall chimney. The bread oven is also still *in situ*; so is the cellar, which has now been made very habitable.

The one remaining inn, the *Red Lion,* was formerly called *The Travellers Arms.* The present building replaces a timber-framed house which was burnt down in 1910.

The *Red Lion* and the *New* inns were in competition at one time, but by 1913, at the latest, the *New* inn had become a private house.

Chapter Twenty-Seven

THE CHURCH

THE CHURCH which we see today, once dedicated to St. John the Baptist, and now called All Saints', incorporates much of the one built by the Benedictine monks of the 12th century. It was carefully rebuilt and added to by the architect George Edmund Street in 1865. The chancel, with its lovely reredos depicting the crucifixion, was the gift of Sir Henry Williams Baker, the vicar who initiated the church's restoration. The earlier chancel (*c.* 1830) was poor, having no chancel-arch; it retained nothing of the original chancel, and so was completely demolished. In the demolition, the original foundations were discovered, as also the remains of a good two-light window of early 14th-century character built up in the walls. This window was carefully copied and inserted in the south wall and later filled with stained glass depicting the Shepherd of the 23rd Psalm. The stained glass in the east window is the work of Hardman and is said to be one of his most successful efforts; in the centre it depicts our Lord in glory, with the saints 'harping with their harps' on either side, and a very happy group of earthly singers singing from a book on the bough of a tree, with shepherds piping below, and angels with different musical instruments above. The whole design accords not only with the dedication of the church, but with the objects of the compilers of *Hymns Ancient and Modern*, by whom it was given.

The nave was rebuilt on the old foundations, but every wrought stone was put back in its former place. Four of the deeply embrasured Norman windows with their tufa surrounds were retained, two in the north and two in the south wall. The other tufa-surrounded windows—the westernmost of the north wall (an Early English lancet) and the central two-light window of the south wall—are the rebuilt windows of the church as Street found it. The jambs of the south doorway are also of tufa, and it, too, is of the 13th century. This use of tufa has been remarked upon as unusual, but it is not unique even in Herefordshire, for the 12th-century church of Moccas is built completely of that material. The picturesque tower of Monkland is characteristic of the 13th and 14th centuries, and the spire is shingled with large broaches.

The charming lych-gate near which Sir H. Williams Baker and his sister are buried was built in 1892 as a memorial to him and was designed by G. E. Street. The cross with a representation of the Good Shepherd, which commemorates the celebrated vicar, has the inscription:

> + Here lieth the body of +
> Henry Williams Baker Bart
> son of Henry L. Baker Bart
> of Richmond, Surrey.

> For 25 years Vicar of this parish who fell
> asleep Feb. 12 A.D. 1877 aged 55 years.

> + Lord all pitying Jesu blest
> Grant him thine eternal rest +.

Beneath this was added later:

> Here lieth the body of Jessy Baker
> Daughter of Henry Lorraine Baker Bart
> of Richmond, Surrey, who entered into her rest
> May 5th 1907, aged 81.
> May the Lord grant her a joyful resurrection.

Within the church on the north side of the chancel floor there is a memorial brass to Sir Henry Baker, showing him in mass vestments.

The church records date from about 1590 and they are written in English up to 1671, when Latin was used until 1743.

SKETCHES MADE BY THOMAS DINGLEY (d. 1695). HISTORY
FROM MARBLE

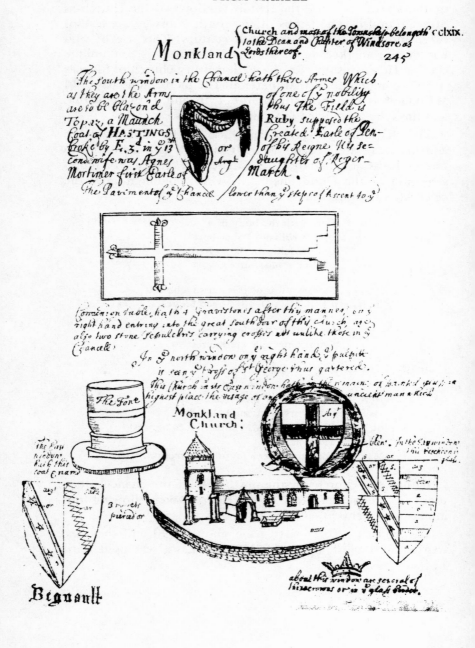

Vicars of Monkland

Date of Institution	Name	Presented by
1289	William de la Ford	Abbey of Conches
1336	Walter de Grawecombe[1]	
1342	Richard fitz Richard of Pembridge	
1349	Walter de Monklone	The King for Conches Abbey
1385	William[2]	
1386	Thomas Bernard[3]	The King (for Conches)
1387	Alexander Clerkes	
1396	Hugh Pontesbury	The King (for Conches)
	Richard Baker	
1411	Adam Skelton	Queen Joan
1413	William Potter	
1417	John Chyrch (or Churche)	The King
1431	Walter Harold	
1433	Hugh Tavener	Roland Leinthale
1436	Thomas Seys	Roland Leinthale
1438	Geoffrey Glasse	Roland Leinthale
	John Greneway[4]	
1483	Richard Gloucestre	Richard Lenthall
	Richard Page	
1524	Richard Benson[5]	Sir Thomas Cornwall
1528	Simon Todde	The King
1531	Richard Kynnerdesley (or Kinnersley)	Sir Thomas Cornwall
1532	John Dyrant	Sir Thomas Cornwall
1537	John Browne	Deans and Canons of Windsor
1546	John Bylthe	Deans and Canons of Windsor
1556	John Busbe	
1595	-. Turbot	
1604	William Tomkins	
1627	William Bedford[6]	All presentations since 1537
1689	James Bedford	have been made by the
1729	Richard Hudson	Deans and Canons of Wind-
1754	Samuel Ford	sor
1780	John Thomas	
1808	Jelinger Symons	
1851	Henry Williams Baker	
1877	William H. Bernard	
1888	John Padfield	
1904	H. N. Midwinter	
1914	Vacant	
1915	A. G. W. Rushton	
1918	Charles E. Whitcombe	
1921	George Walter	
1960	L. F. L. Bannister	
1965	John Clingo	

There are a few gaps in the record. The bishops' registers reveal no institutions between 1349 and 1385, and between 1436 and 1483, though the resignation of John Greneway, Richard Gloucestre's predecessor, is recorded. Richard Page, whose institution is not recorded, may have had a predecessor following Richard Gloucestre. After 1536 the list is probably complete, though we cannot be sure because (1) the register of Bishop Herbert Westphaling (1569-1601) has been lost: (2) some registers were carelessly kept—during Robert Bennett's episcopacy (1602-1617) no institution is entered for eight successive years; (3) no institution is recorded for the period of the Civil War (1636-1661).

It will be observed in the list that on the death of Richard Page in 1542, Sir Thomas Cornwall presented Richard Benson to the living, and he was duly instituted by Bishop Bothe. Cornwall was claiming the right of presentation as the heir of the Lenthalls, but the Crown disputed this claim and established its own right to appoint vicars to Monkland. The Bishop was ordered to institute the King's nominee, Simon Todde, in 1528. Yet Richard Benson did not resign the living until 1531, and when he did, Sir Thomas Cornwall presented Richard Kynnerdesley and, when he died in 1532, John Dyrant. It would appear that Monkland had two vicars until March 1538 when Simon Todde resigned and the Deans and Canons of Windsor presented John Browne. No record of the resignation or death of John Dyrant is available. The King had granted the right of presentation to the lords of the manor, the Dean and Canons of the Royal Chapel at Windsor, with whom it has rested ever since.

Notes on Certain Vicars of Monkland

1. Bishop Thomas Charlton (1327-1343) issued a mandate to cause Walter de Grawecombe to appear before the justices of York to answer the plea of John de Mershton, who claimed from him a debt of £36.

2. Bishop John Gilbert (1375-1389) empowered the rector of Kingsland (Roger Nasshe) to enquire into the alleged immorality of the parson of Monkland (one William) and to impose due punishment.

3. Bishop Gilbert licensed the rector of Monkland, Thomas Bernard, to farm the profits of his benefice to Sir Richard Talbot, for five years during his absence, but Bernard resigned and the King as patron

(replacing the Abbey of Conches) presented Alexander Clerkes to replace him (clergy were frequently given leave of absence to study at various universities).

4. John Greneway was a canon of Hereford and an ecclesiastical commissioner of some distinction. He was appointed Canon and Prebendary of Pratum Minor in April 1462. In April 1466 he resigned the prebend of the Pratum Minor when accepting that of Warham. The date of his appointment to the vicarage of Monkland is not known, but he resigned it in August 1483 and died in 1486.

5. In the register of Bishop Bothe it is possible to trace the career of Richard Benson. It repays attention, for it gives some idea of the mobility of the pre-Reformation clergy.

He is first mentioned as being instituted to the chantry of the Blessed Virgin Mary at Leominster in 1515, presented by the Abbot and Convent of Reading on the nomination of 12 men of Leominster. He resigned from this post in 1518 to take up a similar one as chaplain to the chantry of Agnes Beaupé in Ludlow church, presented to that by Oliver Beaupé. Three years later in 1521, with the approval of Nicholas Vaws or Vaux, he was instituted rector of Richards Castle. In 1524 the Bishop made him one of the executors of the will of Richard Page, who, as vicar of Monkland, had recently died. Benson then succeeded Page as vicar, presented to the living by Sir Thomas Cornwall. He continued to hold this office in spite of the Bishop's institution of the King's nominee Todde in 1528, until 1531, when he resigned. While vicar of Monkland, he continued to be rector of Richards Castle, for in 1527 he was appointed as such to a commission together with Roger Hunt and Richard King, chaplains celebrating in Ludlow church, 'to take charge of clerks arraigned before lay-judges within the diocese and to commit them to the Bishop's gaol'.

In 1536 Richard Benson was Third Portioner in the church of Burford of which his good friend Sir Thomas Cornwall was patron. In 1537 he resigned and was given a pension of four marks per annum.

6. From 4 July 1627 to 11 December 1689 William Bedford was minister of the church of Monkland. He was succeeded by his son James, who was minister until 28 March 1729. Thus father and son were ministers of the church of Monkland for 101 years, 8 months, 3 weeks and 3 days.

The Puritan survey of the parish in 1642 describes Mr. Bedford as 'a seldome preacher', and Monkland as a vicarage worth £100 per annum.

Monkland Curates

Some vicars appear never to have functioned in their church, as their names do not occur in the registers as baptising, marrying or burying any parishioners. They, no

doubt, drew the income from their office and paid a curate
to act for them; most of the work at Monkland from 1754
to 1851 was done by curates. The following have been
culled from the registers:

1732–1734	Richard Davies
1734–1739	Robert Lewis
1740–1742	Richard Coke and John Evans
1744–1759	Joseph Carless
1760	Ben Lawrence
1760–1769	Lewis Beynon
1769	John Thomas (appointed vicar 1780)
1809–1814	Evan Evans
1815–1831	James Powell
1833–1851	W. E. Evans

Other clergymen officiating at Monkland ceremonies from
time to time were : W. Cooke, 1815; Rev. Mr. Whitney,
1831; Rev. Ed. Benyon, 1836; Rev. T. Vernon, 1845–45;
Rev. C. Stapleton, 1847; Rev. C. Scratchley, 1847; Rev.
Evans (former curate?), 1849–50; J. Bowell, 1850 (presumably James Powell, former curate); W. E. Scarf, 1850; W.
Perminster, 1851.

Monkland Recusancy

In the 17th century, when there was a great deal of
residual Catholicism in Herefordshire, Monkland was almost
wholly conformist. The only 'popish recusants' I have traced
in the parish are Catherine Gayne, who was called upon to
take the oath in 1678, and John Aubrey, gent., who was
reported to the bishop as 'a recusant and a repugner of the
truth in Christian religion' (his wife was also a recusant).
In addition, in 1634 it was reported that one Elizabeth Gaine
'doth not resort to church'.

The well-known recusant family of Blount of Orleton
seems to have had property in Monkland in the 16th century.
Richard Blount of Monkland died without children, but his
heir seems to have been Roger Blount of Grendon, called
also 'of Monkland'. He married Mary Berington of Winsley
and their sixth son was Miles Blount of Orleton, who died

in 1663 and is buried in Orleton church. His eldest son was the great Herefordshire antiquary, Thomas Blount.

By the 18th century many of the old stalwarts of Catholicism had given up the wearisome struggle, and had conformed for the sake of peace and quiet, but in 1767 the vicar of Monkland, the Rev. Samuel Ford, when called upon to supply the names of any recusants in his parish, wrote from Ross to the Bishop as follows: 'Thomas Caldwall, a reputed Papist of the Farm of Monkland, aged about 40, has been resident in the parish for about 12 years'.

Monkland had its Protestant recusants, too; in 1678 Thomas Gwilliam and his wife were presented as Quakers.

Values of Several Ecclesiastical Properties as shown by Tax Assessments

In 1488, Convocation granted a subsidy of £25,000 to the King (Henry VII), and the churches and parishes of the diocese were assessed for their shares. A comparison of a few well known cases show the relative value of the livings.

	£	s.	d.
Priory of Leominster	43	2	11
Priory of Wormesley	2	13	4
Priory of Wigmore	4	8	6
Cathedral of Hereford	38	0	0
Vicarage of Leominster		8	4
Vicarage of Weobley		10	0
Church of Monkland		8	4

In 1505 the second half of an Aid of £12,000 had to be collected for the King from the Church. Here are the amounts which had to be raised from a few churches in the area:

	£	s.	d.
Hereford	345	13	4
Leominster Vicarage		6	8
Monkland church		4	4
Pembridge church		26	8
Kingsland church		20	0
Vicarage of Wigmore		3	4
Vicarage of Sarnesfield		3	4

Chapter Twenty-Eight

ECCLESIASTICAL DEVELOPMENTS

LIKE MOST ANGLICAN parish priests before the passing of the Tithe Commutation Act of 1836 and its amending Acts, the vicar of Monkland derived his income from the tithes of the produce of the farmers of Monkland. For the benefit of the Commissioners the value of these tithes was assessed in 1840 and amounted to the surprisingly high sum of £250 15s. 0d.

The figures the valuers used are of interest in showing what the main crops were, and the prices they fetched on the market.

Crop	Price per bushel		No. of bushels in units and decimals
	s.	d.	
Wheat	7	0½	238.10088
Barley	3	11½	422.31578
Oats	2	9	607.87878

In the agreement for the commutation of the tithes between 'the several bodies politic and 40 persons owning land in Monkland . . . and the Rev. Gelinger Symons as Endowed Vicar', it was established that the vicar should receive an annual sum of £250 15s. 0d. by way of a rent charge (subject to the provisions of the Act and subject to the variations in respect of the charge upon hop grounds). I expect this substitution of a money rent for real goods has proved very detrimental to the former farmers of the tithes, for this income will have declined in value just as the charity incomes did.

The vicarage we see today was built in 1894 to replace another which had been burnt down in the previous year. It cost more than £2,400, of which the Ecclesiastical Commissioners gave £1,500.

By 1851 the effects of the revival in the Church of England, inspired by the Tractarians, made themselves felt in Monkland. The parish clergy had duly baptised, married and buried their parishioners, but their celebrations of the Communion had been limited to the three feasts of Christmas, Easter and Whitsuntide. Presumably they read or sang mattins and evensong and preached on Sundays, but evidence of this is not available. After 1851, however, the parishioners were to be surprised.

On 6 February 1851, we find the vicar, the Rev. Jelinger Symons, present at the parish vestry meeting. This in itself was an innovation, but the meeting was called to consider a plan, no doubt issuing from the vicar, 'for erecting a gallery for the removal of the Organ and Singers from the Communion rails as well as a Vestry for the use of the Minister and Meetings of this Parish'. It was agreed that the plan should be carried out, provided that the cost should not fall on the ratepayers. They did not know what was coming.

The Rev. Henry Williams Baker succeeded Jelinger Symons in 1851, and from the beginning of 1852 took the chair at vestry meetings. He was determined to make great changes, and to set about winning over the officers to his point of view. His plan to celebrate the Holy Communion much more frequently led to his demand for six bottles of wine for this purpose. The officers decided that four was enough. In May 1854 the vestry found it necessary to set limits to the expenditure on wine, washing of surplices and church cleaning.

On 24 July 1851 the vestry had agreed to levy a rate of twopence in the pound for necessary repairs to the church. In June 1853 the churchwardens proposed a rate of fourpence in the pound for the repairs of the church and the wall around it.

In October 1864 a much more thorough restoration was thought to be necessary, and the following resolution was carried: 'We . . . being the major part of the Inhabitants

and Occupiers assessed . . . in the Parish of Monkland in
Vestry assembled do hereby resolve and determine that the
sum of money which is requisite for the purpose of repairing
the Church amounts to £400, and we direct and consent
that the Churchwardens and Overseers do . . . make application to the Commissioners of Public Works for a Loan of
£250—part of the sum requisite'.

The loan was obtained, and for years afterwards the parish
was paying back capital and interest by levying a rate. In
1874 the debt still outstanding was £18. It was not finally
paid off until 1885.

The Rev. Sir. H. W. Baker's custom of presiding at the
parish vestry was continued by his successors. His immediate
successor, the Rev. W. H. Barnard, was followed by the
Rev. John Padfield who first took the chair at the vestry
in April 1890. In July 1899, after opening the meeting
with prayer, he explained why no churchwarden had been
appointed at the Easter vestry—it was because no one had
attended. He was clearly at loggerheads with his congregation; he impressed upon the meeting that those who were
appointed as churchwardens were bound to attend to their
duties and take the collections. He then defended himself
against attacks made upon him by a gentleman of the parish.

In Easter 1904 no vestry was held because there was no
vicar to take the chair; it appears that the old democracy
had given way to autocracy!

The Rev. H. M. Midwinter took the chair as vicar in
Easter 1905. At the vestry of 1907 Mrs. M. Edwards was
chosen as churchwarden, and she was joined by Mr. W. Cave
as second churchwarden in 1910. From that period onwards
the Edwards family and the Misses Moody became very
prominent as parish workers, as has been mentioned in
'Mrs. Speakman's Recollections'; Miss Grace Moody raised
money for the repair of the steeple, for example. The three
sisters lived at Horkesley House, the former home of Sir
H. W. Baker, and shared something of the former vicar's
enthusiasm for the church, for they were behind all parish
activities. They ran the Band of Hope and conducted evening
classes, and Gertrude taught wood-carving to the parish

youth. The boys carved the backs of chairs, which were bought by the parishioners for the church at 2s. 6d. each to commemorate the Coronation of George V in 1911, and have the monogram 'GR V̄' carved on the top. The work of these wood-carvers is still to be found in houses around Monkland, and Mrs. Dorothy Speakman possesses a fine chest decorated by the boys of Miss Gertrude's wood-carving class, which was conducted in the Manor Farm.

The Rev. Charles Whitcombe became vicar in 1917, when Miss Mary Moody and Mr. George Lewis were his church-wardens. In 1919 the vestry thought it advisable to reintroduce *Hymns Ancient and Modern*, which had surprisingly been superseded at some stage after Sir H. W. Baker's incumbency. At this meeting the Misses Moody received sincere thanks for their faithful services to church and parish. It was not, however, before the incumbency of the Rev. G. Walker in 1922 that the famous hymnal, which had to a great extent been compiled in Monkland, was again used in the church.

In 1945 Wing-Commander and Mrs. Nigel Bengough appear among the officers of the church, and thereafter 'Captain' Bengough, as People's Warden, regularly presented the church accounts for many years.

During the Rev. G. Walter's incumbency (1922-1960) the parish became united with the parish of Ivington, of which Mr. Walter had been vicar since 1916. The Right of Presentation to the United Benefices is now made alternately by the Dean and Canons of Windsor and the vicar of Leominster. Upon Rev. G. Walter's retirement, the Dean and Canons of Windsor expressed a desire to confer with the churchwardens about the appointment of a new vicar. The Dean said he had offered the living to four clergymen, all of whom had declined it, one objection being the size of the vicarage. Further, the incumbent of a country parish needed a car. In 1959 at a joint meeting of Ivington and Monkland church councils, Mr. E. W. Speakman had proposed that the vicar should be allowed £1 a week car allowance. During his incumbency the Rev. G. Walter had kept the church locked to avoid thefts; though the parishioners had objected, the vicar had been supported by the churchwardens.

In 1960 the Rev. L. F. L. Bannister was appointed Vicar of the United Benefice, and the 'care' of Upper Hill (in the parish of Hope under Dinmore) was added to his charge. In 1961 the vicarage was partly demolished and the remainder modernised. In 1965 the present vicar, the Rev. John Clingo, succeeded the Rev. L. F. L. Bannister.

22. The Lych Gate, Monkland, a memorial to the Rev. Sir Henry Baker.

21. The Cruck House, originally the *Seven Stars* Inn, Monkland.

23. Horkesley House, Monkland, formerly the home of Sir Henry Williams Baker.

24. Monkland's former school.

25. The church of St.
Mary the Virgin,
Eardisland.

26. Interior view of St. Mary's church, Eardisland.

27.   Burton Court, Eardisland.

28.   The building on the left is the old school; on the right the old Court House, Eardisland.

29. Manor House, Eardisland, previous names of which were Vulkan House and Porch House. The origins of the present name are not known.

30. The whipping post, Eardisland, under the window of the old school.

31. Gethin's Arrow bridge and the old school, Eardisland.

32. The moated mound or fortress, Eardisland.

Chapter Twenty-Nine

SIR HENRY WILLIAMS BAKER, Bart.

IT IS DUE to the fame of this 19th-century vicar that the tiny and obscure village of Monkland is far better known than other villages of its size. While Sir H. W. Baker was the spiritual pastor of Monkland for over twenty-five years, the village was much frequented by his clerical and musical friends. These visits were facilitated by the building of the railway which connected Leominster with the national network when the Shrewsbury–Hereford line was opened in 1853. It was Sir Henry who was the dynamic leader of the several distinguished men who compiled that anthology of hymns known as *Hymns Ancient and Modern,* which rapidly gained popularity and is still widely used more than a century after its first publication.

The Rev. Sir H. W. Baker was born on 17 May 1821. He was the eldest and last surviving son of Vice-Admiral Sir Henry Loraine Baker and his wife, Louisa Anne, only daughter of Mr. William Williams, sometime M.P. for Weymouth. (Note the Welsh connection perpetuated in Sir Henry's name.)

He was educated at Trinity College, Cambridge, where he graduated as a B.A. in 1844 and and M.A. in 1847. After ordination he acted as curate at Great Horkesley in Essex until he was appointed vicar of Monkland in 1851.

A nephew of the Rev. W. Edwards, who was vicar of Orleton at that time, writes that his uncle (who had also been a curate at Great Horkesley) and Baker were rivals for the hand of the same young lady, Miss Laetitia Bonner. (The east windows of Orleton church were filled with stained glass in her memory.) When she eventually chose Mr. Edwards, the nephew writes, 'there was no further friendly communication between the vicarages of Orleton and Monkland'. Baker, in fact, remained a bachelor, and was later well known as an advocate of the celibacy of the clergy.

When Sir Henry arrived in Monkland there was no vicarage, so he had one built to his own designs, calling it 'Horkesley House' after the place of his curacy, which suggests that he had many happy memories of his first clerical post. The house was provided with a private chapel, in which the organ was a prominent piece of furniture; in fact the vicar's love of sacred music was so great that all the members of his staff, indoors and outdoors, were chosen for their ability to sing in the choir. Baker was himself a competent amateur musician, and shortly after arriving in Monkland he wrote his earliest hymn, 'Oh, what, if we are Christ's, is earthly shame or loss?'.

The drive for which Sir H. W. Baker was noted was manifested very early in his Monkland pastorate, for he quickly set about providing the village with a school. A parcel of glebe land belonging to the vicarage was conveyed by him, with the consent of Bishop Renn Dickson Hampden and the Dean and Canons of Windsor, as a site for the school on 12 May 1852. Once in operation the new National School, which had places for 60 children, soon won a reputation for efficiency.

The church was in a dilapidated condition when the new vicar started his incumbency, so as soon as he was able he applied his efforts to its restoration. He commissioned one of the best architects of his day to examine and report on it. This man, George Edmund Street (who was later responsible for the Law Courts in London, and the restoration of the cathedrals of York, Salisbury and Carlisle) was not very well known in 1865 when Baker employed him for this purpose. Street recommended a thorough rebuilding, although, as has been mentioned, he eventually managed to preserve some of the earlier features of the church. Part of the cost of this work was covered by a loan of £250 granted by the Public Works Loan Commissioners. In a letter of 3 August 1865 Baker makes himself responsible for the repayment of this loan: 'Whatsoever is not subscribed I am quite willing to pay'.

The work was completed in 1866 and the reopening was carried out with great solemnity. Baker composing for the occasion his famous hymn, 'Lord Thy word abideth', which found a place in later editions of *Hymns Ancient and Modern.*

Like John Mason Neale, also a graduate of Trinity College Cambridge, Sir Henry was an enthusiastic convert to the Oxford Movement, led by Newman and Pusey, which stressed the Catholicism of the Church of England. Both were in trouble from time to time for their ritualistic practices, which were seen by ultra-Protestants as 'popish'. They were both keen on providing the Church of England with a hymn-book to accompany its liturgy. Cranmer, who had translated the liturgy and created the Prayer Book, had omitted to supply the hymns with which the ancient service books had been liberally sprinkled. Neale was especially gifted as a translator of Latin hymns, a fact which is demonstrated by the large number of these in *Hymns Ancient and Modern.*

In 1858 Sir Henry was engaged on a scheme for amalgamating the best hymns in rival collections. The interested parties met in the clergy-house of St. Barnabas, Pimlico, where G. C. White, the editor of *Hymns and Introits,* was curate-in-charge. Some of the writers wanted almost the whole of *Hymns Ancient and Modern* to consist of translations from the Latin. When the first edition of the collection appeared in 1861 the treasures of ancient Latin hymnody were in considerable evidence, but to ensure a favourable reception for the book the compilers added many modern hymns.

In compiling *Hymns Ancient and Modern,* Baker was ably assisted by the musical editor, Professor W. H. Monk, the Rev. J. B. Dykes, vicar of St. Oswald's Durham, composer of many of the tunes, and Sir Frederick Arthur Gore Ouseley, who had founded the famous musical college of St. Michael's, Tenbury, in 1857; yet Sir Henry had a remarkable critical faculty which seemed to dictate to him the probable future of a hymn tune. He was also able to try it out with his

carefully-chosen and trained village choir. The much-loved
hymn 'The King of love my Shepherd is' was written in 1868
and published in the same year as an appendix to his hymnal.
Baker is said to have composed the first tune to the words,
but as it was not very successful he sent his verses to his
friend, J. B. Dykes, who wrote the tune which has made
the hymn so popular: 'Dominus regit me'. A good deal of
anger was expressed in many quarters over the charming
hymn which Sir Henry composed in honour of the Blessed
Virgin Mary: 'Shall we not love thee, Mother dear, Whom
Jesus loves so well'. One had to have a broad back in those
days to give Mary due honour within the Church of England.
A copy of the first edition of *Hymns Ancient and Modern*
(now in Leominster museum) used in the church of
Pudleston has the following expressions crossed out as
objectionable: the refrain 'Jesu, Son of Mary hear', in the
hymn (163) 'When our heads are bowed with woe'. It is
substituted with 'Jesu, Son of God give ear'. 'Be present
Son of Mary' in verse 5 of John Keble's 'The Voice that
breathed o'er Eden', is substituted with 'Be present, Holy
Jesus'.

Professor Monk used occasionally to stay at Horkesley
House as Sir Henry's Guest. When he played the church
organ—the best in Herefordshire at that time, that of the
Cathedral alone excepted—the organ blower complained
of the hard work he had because Monk 'used such a lot of
wind'. When he did not play he sat in the tower at the west
end of the church, where he snored audibly during the
sermon. Thus it is said that he made a great noise at which-
ever end of the church he happened to be.

In Sir Henry's time the choir was noted for its excellence.
The choirmaster for a large area of Herefordshire lived in
the parish; he had an admirable voice, and both he and his
wife were good organists (his wife was the better so he
replaced her only when necessary).

With Dr. Monk Sir Henry was also responsible for the
production of 'The Psalter pointed and set to accompanying
Chants, "Ancient and Modern".' It was not published until
after Sir Henry's death and Dr. Monk opens the preface

with these words: 'This Psalter pointed and set to accompanying Chants "ancient and modern" is the result of earnest thought and editorial labour extending over many years. Sir Henry Baker entered upon the work with the same energy and unwearied devotion which he had given in the preparation of "Hymns Ancient and Modern" and it was almost his dying wish that he might witness and assist in its completion. But it was God's will to remove him from the Church on earth when the end seemed well nigh accomplished'.

Sir Henry's last address to his people, dictated from what proved to be his death-bed, was printed in his Parish Magazine, and well illustrates his characteristic devotion and his deep love for those to whom he ministered. The letter, dated 30 January 1877, is headed 'My dear friends and children in Jesus Christ', and reads as follows:

> I little thought when I wrote to you on New Year's Day how soon I should be more ill than I had been. But it pleased God within two days to lay me low by an attack of acute rheumatism, and it is only within the last day or two that I have been able even to leave my bed; and they say that if I am able to move a few weeks hence it will be quite necessary for me to have change of air and entire rest for two or three months. So the Confirmation must be postponed (but the Bishop has most kindly said that he will still come here as soon as I shall have been able to prepare the candidates), and I shall have to spend Lent and possibly Easter away from you. This will be very trying both to you and me; and yet I hope you will heartily thank God for what He has done. I feel as if I could never thank Him enough for myself: first, for having sent me His fatherly correction; and, secondly, for having dealt so very gently and tenderly with me through it. And if I come back to work among you again, perhaps we shall see that it has been 'well'. I thank you so much for the sympathy and affection which has made so many of you come or send to the house to ask how I was; and especially I thank those of you who have been regular at Holy Communion, and have remembered me in your prayers there. If you care for me, be often at the Lord's Table; and as you think of the dying love of Jesus, ask God that He would give both to me and yourselves the grace that we most need, for His dear sake.
>
>   Believe me always,
>   Your affectionate Pastor,
>   Henry W. Baker.

To illustrate the hymnologist's character and the esteem in which he was held both by his friends and parishioners I cannot do better than quote the words of the *Herefordshire Journal* shortly after his death in Monkland on 12 February 1877. As he died he was heard repeating verses 1 and 3 of 'The King of love'. Verse 3 begins 'Perverse and foolish oft I strayed'.

> Not only among those musicians who had the good fortune to hold intercourse with him will his hearty warmth and genuine affection be ever missed, but also by the comfortless widow, the aged, and the orphans in that small parish which was his home. With every face he was familiar, sympathised with every suffering heart, joyed in every smile; and no dissentients did he find to the beautiful forms of divine worship carried out in his church after his own liking, because all who knew him were drawn to him by his simplicity and purity of character, and loved him with that love which casteth out fear.

The gracious hostess of Horkesley House was his loving and devoted sister, Jessy, who was five years younger than he. She died at Worthing in 1907 at the age of 81 and was brought back to Monkland to be buried beside her brother.

The funeral of Sir Henry Williams Baker was reported in the *Herefordshire Journal* of 17 February 1877, together with the following tribute to his general goodness:

> The beautifully restored church with its excellent choir and crowded services, the efficient school, and indeed every department of the parochial machinery bear witness to the successful zeal of the late vicar and his devotion to the duties of his sacred calling. His memory will live long in the grateful recollection of the people of Monkland whom he loved so well and for whose good he laboured so heartily up to the beginning of his short illness.

Two memorials were dedicated to the memory of the Rev. Sir H. W. Baker. In 1878 a stained glass window was inserted in the south wall of the church chancel, and in 1893 a lychgate was erected at the entrance to the churchyard.

A memorial brass showing him in mass vestments was placed in the floor on the north side of the chancel, bearing the words: 'To the Glory of God and the grateful and affectionate remembrance of their Chairman Henry Williams Baker Bart., for 25 years the faithful Vicar of this parish this memorial is placed by his surviving colleagues in the compilation of Hymns Ancient and Modern.   R.I.P.'

A Schoolmaster in Monkland. 1665

There is no evidence of a school in the village before the establishment of the National School during the incumbency of the Rev. Sir H. W. Baker. The bishop licensed schoolmasters, but there is no evidence that one was licensed for Monkland. Boys from the parish whose parents were appreciative of education would have gone, no doubt, to the grammar schools in the neighbouring parishes of Eardisland or Kingsland. Yet a manuscript in Hereford Cathedral Library reveals that one John Gower was in trouble with the Dean and Chapter of Hereford for teaching poor children to read—he was probably teaching without a licence. It is a directive from Bishop Herbert Croft to the Dean and Chapter:

> Whereas I am informed that the bearer hereof, John Gower of Munckland is cited into the Court for teaching poore children to read. These are therefore to require you that you dismisse him without any costs or molestation, and that you forbeare giving any other persons molestation for the future in that behalfe. Given under my hand this 6th of March 1665.
>
> Her. Hereford.

(The Gowers were fairly numerous in Monkland in the 17th century, and this could be the John Gower who was churchwarden with Walter Sheward in 1665.)

Chapter Thirty

A FEW STATISTICS

Population

1821	..	..	187	1911	..	..	206
1831	..	..	180	1921	..	..	187
1841	..	..	185	1931	..	..	166
1851	..	..	179	1951	..	..	183
1891	..	..	207	1961	..	..	170
1901	..	..	204	1974	..	..	138

Baptisms

1783	..	..	6	1852	..	..	4
1784	..	..	7	1853	..	..	7
1786	..	..	4	1854	..	..	6
1787	..	..	5	1855	..	..	9
				1856	..	..	6

Communicants

1872	..	..	43	1913	..	..	43
1879	..	..	61	1920	..	..	42
1886	..	..	65	1950	..	..	45
				1973	..	..	41

EARDISLAND

Erdestland Church.

Here is little of Antiquity except this monument adjoining to the wall of the seat of Mr Brewster of Burton without Inscripcon. on the top onely are seen y coats following and the Device marked A

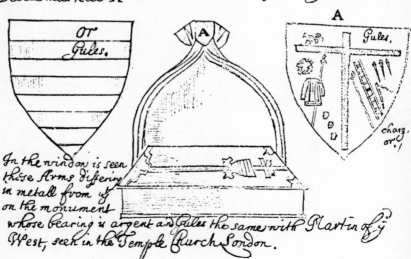

Or Gules.

A

Gules.

charg. or.

In the window is seen these Arms differing in metall from y on the monument whose bearing is argent and Gules the same with Martin of y West, seen in the Temple Church London.

FOREWORD

Leominster, the Minster of the Leon or Lene

THE VILLAGE whose history is recounted in the following pages forms part of an area in north-west Herefordshire anciently called the Leon or Lene, of which the chief town in Leominster.

Leominster became important because it was chosen, possibly in ancient British times, but certainly in very early Saxon times, as the site of a monastery which was amply endowed with lands. Outside the precinct of this religious house grew up a secular manufacturing and trading community which provided the market for the agricultural communities surrounding it.

During the stormy centuries of the Saxon period the town suffered frequent devastations owing to its position on the border of Wales, but after the establishment in Norman times by Henry I of the Benedictine Priory of monks —a cell of the great Abbey of Reading—Leominster had a more ordered existence, the town outside the Priory growing in wealth and importance to such an extent that it rivalled Hereford, and from 1297 onwards, it was represented in Parliament by two Members.

The dissolution of the Priory under Henry VIII, though not welcomed, did little to check the prosperity of the town, which remained the metropolis of north-west Herefordshire up to the middle of the 19th century. Then, owing to the impact of the Industrial Revolution, improved communications with the rest of the country, and free trade, it fell into decline. Now, at last, it shows signs of new life, and begins to appreciate its heritage of buildings and traditions.

For a detailed account of the fascinating history of Leominster, see the author's *The Town in the Marches*.

127

INTRODUCTION

OF THE THREE '-land' villages, Eardisland is the most picturesque. Some have regarded it as the prettiest village in the county. Its charm is an accidental product of its situation and its former poverty, which for centuries inhibited any extensive rebuilding or expansion. In recent years its inhabitants have appreciated the value of their legacy from the past and have exerted themselves to preserve it unspoilt.

Eardisland, pronounced locally *a:dslaend*, grew up round a crossing of the River Arrow. It lies between the crossing upstream at Pembridge, 3km. to the west, and that downstream at Monkland, 4-5km. to the south-east. The important road which passes through it (the A44) connects Leominster with Kington and Wales.

The Anglian prince of the Magonsaete, Merewalh, son of the mighty Mercian king Penda, after establishing his religious house at Leominster, on the west bank of the River Lugg, pushed gradually further westwards among the then apparently friendly Welsh into a fertile area called the Leon which was drained by the rivers, Arrow, Pinsley and Lugg. As mentioned earlier the name denotes 'The flowing waters', so marked a feature of the area, being derived from the root *lei* ('to flow) in Welsh *lliant*. The element is preserved in the '-land' of our three villages, in the name of an ancient farm in Pembridge, the Leen, and in Lyonshall, called in Domesday Book 'Lenehalle'. The chief town in the area grew up round the monastic settlement, the Leon-minster.

The Leon was later sub-divided into the areas which give their names to the villages. The King retained a part for himself, the monks of the abbey of Conches in Normandy were endowed with Monkland, and Earl Morcar acquired

Eardisland, the Earlslene which appears in Domesday Book as Orleslene, from Old English *eorl*, 'earl'.

The low lying villages of Kingsland, Monkland and Eardisland were exposed to attacks from the Welsh from the hillier west, who came raiding for cattle and sheep. To afford some protection from these the Rowe Ditch, an earthwork running roughly north–south just west of Pembridge, and visible still on the Leen farm, was built. This was supplemented later by Offa's Dyke on the western boundary of the Leon, near Lyonshall. Later still, perhaps, rose the castles at Lyonshall, Weobley and Dilwyn. Kingsland and Eardisland acquired their own moated fortresses, now to be seen as mounds just west of their respective churches. Eardisland's 'motte' is still surrounded by a water-filled moat.

The Manor of Eardisland was granted, together with other lands, to Ralph de Todeni. Lord Rennell of Rodd, who has concerned himself a great deal with this area, thinks that the Domesday manor probably lay south of the present village, which, lying at the river crossing, is very low. He suggests that the house of the lord of the 15-hide manor was either at the moated mound or on the higher ground at Burton, 1.3km. south of the village.

The parish of Eardisland includes two former manors besides that of Eardisland itself: Burton and Hinton.

The three manors were organised in the usual way following the introduction of the feudal system. The inhabitants were ruled by manorial lords who were themselves tenants and vassals of greater lords, who held their vast domains of the King who was the only true landowner. For failure to carry out their obligations to him they could be deprived at any time.

Part of the land of the manor was reserved by the lord as his demesne. His tenants paid for his protection by cultivating this for him, and thus were obliged to spend two or three days of their week working for his steward. The rest of the territory was shared among the tenants. It consisted of large arable fields and waste or common land.

The arable fields, each of which was planted with one crop—wheat, barley, oats or rye—were divided into acre strips. Each peasant was allotted one or more strips in each great field, for the cultivation of which he was responsible. Strips were separated from one another by baulks or 'meres'. To have three arable fields was normal, and the growing of the same crop in a field continually was avoided by rotation. One field was left cropless or 'fallow' every year, so that the soil could recuperate. During this fallow year the farm animals were allowed to graze on the grass and weeds which sprang up on the untilled ground and so manure it.

The management of the manorial farm was carried out by an assembly of the lord and his tenants—the 'court leet', to which the villagers were summoned, under pain of fine for absence, at regular internals. The lord or his steward presided. The court decided the policy of the farm, the times of ploughing, sowing and reaping, the times when fields were open for grazing, and the number of animals each tenant could put into them. The court recorded changes of tenancy as arranged by the customs of the manor. Tenants who had infringed the rules were 'presented', given time to mend gates, and clean out ditches, and fined if they did not do so as bidden within a given time.

As there were within the parish three manors each of these held its own court leet, and each kept its own manorial rolls.

The following extracts illustrate the sort of business transacted by these courts:

> (a) Court Leet and Court Baron of Thomas, Marquis of Bath, Viscount Weymouth . . . Lord of the Manor of Eardisland, held at the usual place, the 22 October 1790, before Robert Whitcombe, Gentleman Steward. Thomas Leinthall of the parish of Letton, a customary tenant of the Manor, surrendered arable land called Lidgoores Cross Croft, 2½ acres towards Burton Court on the north and east and lands of William Trumper gent. on the south, and Thomas Leinthall was admitted as his nephew and next Customary Heir of Thomas Leinthall, formerly of Hardwick in the parish of Eardisland gent. to the use and behoof of Thomas Cole of the Parish of Pembridge, yeoman.

> (b) Court Leet of Robert Cutler, Lord of the Manor of Hinton held before the Bailiff, John Addis 1715. The Homage [the tenants attending the court] included William Melling gent., Richard Fencott, Thomas Froysell, Thomas Watkins, William Mascall, Thomas Pricket and Thomas Trumper.

'and the Homage alsoe lay a paine of XXXIXs. XId. upon every person or persons who shall tye or turne any manner of cattle within any of the Common Fields belonging to this Manor untill the said fields are fully rid or clensed of the last Sheafe or Cork'.

In 1716 James Owens was fined £39 11s. 0d. for this very offence.

(c) Court Leet of Bryan Crowther, Lord of the Manor of Hinton in 1734.

Thomas Shewheard and Comfort his wife are threatened with a fine of 39s. if they do not cleanse a certain water course.

Also: 'We present Roger Turberville at the Broome estate for Inclosing up part of the Waste land belonging to this manor lying near to the said Brome House with a gate and rails, and also for making a Water course across the roadway there, belonging to this manor.' He must restore this before the next Court or pay a penalty of 39s.

The Court Rolls of the Manor of Burton have some specially interesting details.

It is well known that the Black Death, by greatly reducing the population, made labourers scarce and therefore valuable. Many who had previously been serfs left the manors to which they belonged and sold their labour to anyone who desperately needed their services. They thus became wage labourers, and free men. We find that at the court held at Burton in 1350, 10 holdings were then 'in the hand of the lord', because the tenants and all their heirs had died.

People who owed suit of court and did not attend were fined. Among those presented for this omission of their duty in 1501 was Roger Whitehouse, the vicar of Eardisland; and, in 1629, Robert Robotham D.D. (son-in-law of Bishop Francis Godwin), who in 1607 had bought the estate of Bidney from the Boyles.

In the reigns of Elizabeth I and James I the whole township was presented at the court for its failure to provide stocks, or a ducking pool. On another occasion it was presented for not having a common pound or pinfold. The inhabitants, with certain exceptions, were presented and each fined fourpence for not wearing caps on Sundays: this in Elizabethan times. As late as the first year of James I's

reign the inhabitants were presented for not practising their
shooting with bows and arrows in accordance with the law.
Also in this reign inhabitants were frequently presented at
the court for maintaining strangers in their houses contrary
to the statute (one wonders if some of these were recusant
priests or Catholics on the run, of which Bishop Robert
Bennet in 1616 gives a list in his register).* Those, too who
offended by watering hemp and flax in streams, 'where cattle
doe use to drinke', were presented.

A number of people were presented for erecting cottages,
presumably on common land, and establishing encroachments. One example is enough: *Presentant quod Georgius
Eve erectavit contra formam statuti 31 Eliz. infra manerium
praedictum unum cottagium in quo Jacobus Evans modo
inhabitat.*

The Court Rolls of the Manor of Burton cover the period
from 1332 (5 Edw. III)-1633 (8 Charles I) with occasional
breaks—3, 5, 7 and 15 years respectively. In spite of these
breaks 150 courts are recorded. Ralph de St. Owen was the
first lord of the manor. In 1428 (6 Henry VI) Thomas
Downton was lord, having married Margaret de St. Owen.
In 1500 (Henry VII) the seneschal or steward of the manor
was John Blount, armiger. In 1553 (1 Mary) John Cotes
held his first court as lord of the manor. No further court
was held until 4 Elizabeth, when John Cotes was still lord
and Thomas Salter his seneschal. John Cotes continued as
lord until 1588. His descendants held the title until the
beginning of the reign of Charles I. For a time the manor
seems to have been occupied by a branch of the Crofts of
Croft Castle, but before 1700 it had become the property
of John Brewster, one of whose sons, William, was an M.D.
and a scholar of some eminence. In his will of 1715 Dr.
Brewster gave to All Saints' church, Hereford, most of the
books which now form its chained library. The Brewsters
held Burton up to the end of the 18th century, when the
heiress married William Evans, by whose daughter and

*'A Catalogue of such Recusants as have not place to sojourn or
inhabit, but traggell [*sic*] from place to place.'

heiress, the wife of the Rev. W. E. Evans, the estate was sold in 1863 to John Clowes.

The Manor of Eardisland came from the Mortimers to the Devereuxes. When Robert Devereux, the third Earl of Essex, died in 1646, it passed to the Marchioness of Hertford and thus to the Thynne family, of which the above-mentioned Viscount Weymouth, first Marquis of Bath, was a member. It is doubtful if this busy statesman of George III ever saw his manor of Eardisland, though his permission was sought by the churchwardens in 1757 to enclose some land 'on the Bearwood' for a workhouse which they agreed to build. As this workhouse was not built, it would appear that the leave was not obtained.

Since the Thynnes sold the manor it has passed through various hands, and manorial tenure and any of its surviving privileges were abolished by the Law of Property Act of 1922. No one today lays claim to being lord of the manor of Eardisland. At the date of the Enclosure Act the lord of the manor was John Robert Smythie, a clergyman, who lived at Lynch Court. At the period of Tithe Commutation he was lessee of the tithes. He was still living in 1851. He, Marianne Atherton, and Charles Haywood were the landowners who promoted the Enclosures of 1811. The expenses of the survey and the subsequent allotment of the common lands were paid for by the sale of some of the land.

In the County Record Office in Hereford there is a 1637 report on the 'Boro of Erislande'* which, besides giving the names of the 41 poor people receiving relief, sets out to prove that the parish is very poor: '. . . there are noe howses kept neither to relive the poore nor serve offices, nor beare nor maintaine armes within in our parishe, but the most parte of the dwellers there doe pleade povertie themselves.'

The names of the estates and their owners are given, and these demonstrate that at that time the land of the parish was already largely enclosed in consolidated farms. Besides the three manors of Eardisland, Burton and Hinton, the following estates are mentioned: Nunnhouse, Hardwick,

*British Museum: Portland Loan: Harley Papers, Loan 29/172.

Barrowe, Riducks, Broxhill, Byrches, Nunlande, Twiford and Broome. Most of the owners are styled 'gent.'. Even part of Bearwood, the chief object of the enclosers of 1811, was enclosed as the farm of one Thomas Culcumbe.

Before 1730 the Limes, the Linch, Grove House, the Seaside, the Stitches, the Brouche, Ridimore, the Court House farm and Gallifers Means (owned by Richard Vaughan of the Bearwood) had been added to these.

Hence the intention of the 1811 enclosers to 'allot and award the *residue* of the common and waste lands, common field lands etc.' is understandable.

When the Tithe Commutation of 1841 took place the land was divided up as follows:

Arable	1,909	acres
Meadow or pasture	2,139	,,
Wood	210	,,
Hop ground	50	,,
Vicarial Glebe	22	,,
Common	6	,,

The total acreage of the parish was thus 4,316. By totalling all the areas of fields already enclosed or still genuinely common (i.e., the six acres mentioned above), with names like 'Burton's Common Field', 'Little Common Field', 'Shirl Common Field', 'Common', 'Common Parks', we arrive at a total of just over 35 acres, which represents about 0.8 per cent. of the land.

Some changes in the parish boundaries took place in 1884 when by a Local Government Board Order (No. 15,956) Upper and Lower Barewood were transferred to Dilwyn and a detached part of the parish was added to Weobley. The area of the parish is now 3,633 acres of land and 23 of water.

Chapter Thirty-One

THE CHURCH OF ST. MARY THE VIRGIN

IT IS PROBABLE that Eardisland had a church in Saxon times, and it is likely to have been built entirely of timber, like most of the village churches before the Conquest. The oldest part of our present building dates from *c.* 1200. This is the aisleless nave which was probably the whole of the earliest stone church, which had no chancel. The blocked-up doorway to the east of the south wall was probably the priest's entrance. In the walls of the nave are still four of the original deeply embrasured lancet windows, three of them in the north wall. Larger windows replaced some of the lancets in the south wall early in the 14th century, probably when the chancel was added, thus making the church much lighter. The south porch and the chancel vestry were also built in the 14th century. The recessed arch on the outside of the south wall of the chancel may, according to some writers, have been intended for the tomb of the founder. The medieval tower, which was as wide as the nave, was surmounted by a steeple, as illustrated in Dingley's sketch from the period of Charles II. In 1749 the parish vestry recorded that the steeple was in great decay and 'very ruingous', and that it was impossible to repair it. The churchwardens were requested to apply to the bishop for a licence to pull it down before it wrecked the tower and crushed the nave. Yet it was not until 1759 that the spire was finally taken down. In 1760 Thomas Hooper of Yarpole, who had put in the lowest tender for the work, built the present tower for £155. Though architecturally unpretentious, it is strong and forms an excellent support for the peal of eight bells. Its two floors are reached by ladders.

The bells, broken in a collapse of the tower, were re-cast in the Rudhall foundry at Gloucester in 1728, a lady parishioner defraying the cost.

In 1864 a thorough restoration of the church was undertaken after a Leominster builder, Mr. William Davies, had reported: 'I find the 2 side walls of the Nave very much out of their perpendicular, also the roof drawn in a very unsightly form, and all this I attribute in the first place to the water falling from the roof and sapping the one side of the foundations, thereby causing the walls to sink outside'. He recommended that the old stone tiles should be stripped off and replaced by slates, and that iron guttering with fall pipes should be used to drain off the rain water. He suggested that three and seven-eighths rods should be put through the wall plates across the nave, and well screwed up. He offered to do all this for £156. If his recommendations were carried out, he thought the church would stand for another century. This was in 1861. In 1865 £1,450 was needed for the restoration, and the churchwardens were directed to apply to Public Works for a loan. The bishop and the incumbent applied to the Church Commissioners for a loan of £300. The curate at this time, the Rev. J. H. Bluck, appealed for contributions, and John Clowes, who had just purchased Burton Court, gave £200. Mr. J. Harding of Lynch Court gave £100, and a further £200 was contributed by strangers. Mr. H. Curzon, an architect, was engaged to superintend the restoration. At that time it was intended that the tower should be given a small shingle spire, but this was never done, and the church will never again look like the one Dingley sketched.

Over the centuries the furnishings of the inside of the church underwent considerable changes. After the Reformation lengthy sermons took the place of liturgical and sacramental worship, and the nave of the church was filled with box pews in which the various households could sit more or less privately in draught-free comfort while listening to the exciting eloquence or boring monologue of their preacher. Those who wished could snooze unobserved by their fellow parishioners, and the wealthier class had their private stoves to warm them. In 1738 the vestry ordered the removal of a pew, set up by one John Prichard Mason in the central gangway of the church without the consent of the parishioners (Mr. Mason was by then dead), 'Which Pew is found to be very inconvenient by rendering the Passage too narrow for the convenient carriage of Corps by the same'. In erecting this pew, Mason had displaced 'a Book of Controversy between the established Church and that of Rome' and removed 'a Bench the Clerk used to respond at Communion Service' (this was a parish event which took place four times a year). Book and bench were to be replaced when the pew was taken down, and the wainscot put in the vestry.

In 1827 the church was again fitted with pews, and in December of that year parishioners met to appropriate their new pews and kneelings. I give a few examples of the allotments:

No. 1. Bull Inn. Chas Haywood's present residence, and Hole Lane.

No. 4. Mr. Greenly's Place at Hardwick, the Brooch and Mund's Place at Burton.

No. 10. Benjamin Miles—the Cross Inn and shop opposite Mrs. Pratt's Place.

No. 19. Mr. Smythies, for Servants of Lynch Court.

No. 23. Broom and Twyford.

No. 24 (a corner seat). The Schoolmaster.

No. 25. Servants, Burton Court.

No. 32. The Vicarage.

No. 42. Lynch Court (Smythies).

In 1839 the vicar or curate must have been a good preacher, for the congregation was so large that £25 of the church rate was set aside for the erection of a western gallery. A further £2 was allotted for its painting. This was removed at the restoration of 1864.

In 1919 more considerable alterations were proposed and undertaken. Colonel Clowes of Burton Court appears to have pushed these forward.

The 15th-century screen, which had formerly enclosed a chantry chapel, was removed from the organ chamber and re-positioned in the tower arch. A new organ was erected in the recess on the north side of the chancel. The altar was lengthened by placing on it an 8ft. 6in. wooden slab.

Four ridel posts surmounted by angels were erected to give
it greater dignity. The original floor level of the sanctuary
was reinstated, and it was repaved with stone. The existing
chancel floor was reduced to the level of the nave.

Three pews on each side of the nave towards the chancel
were removed. This portion of the nave and the central
aisle were floored with artificial stone slabs, and the pulpit
and font were moved a few feet forward.

Thus the church achieved its present dignified appearance.

Chapter Thirty-Two

THE CHURCH BELLS

AS HAS BEEN MENTIONED in the account of the church, the medieval bells were broken in a collapse of the tower. When they were recast in 1728, no attempt was made to reproduce the probably interesting inscriptions upon them. It was a time when the educated classes despised and wanted to forget everything which savoured of 'the old superstitions'. The nostalgia for the still recent past had not developed. Hence when A. Rudhall recast the five bells, he gave them new inscriptions:

1. Prosperity to the Church of England   ..   ..   A.R. 1728
2. Peace and good neighbourhood   ..   ..   ..   A.R. 1728
3. Prosperity to this Parish   ..   ..   A.R. 1728
4. I to the Church the Living call, and to the grave
     do summon all..   ..   ..   A.R. 1728
5. Geo. Kinnersley Gt., and Jon Davis, churchwardens   A.R. 1728

In 1906 the bells were re-hung and a treble bell was added. The sum needed for this (£148) was raised by voluntary subscriptions. In 1950 it was found that the oak bell frame had decayed, so the bells were taken out until enough money was raised to put them into working order again. For two years they were silent. Sufficient money was raised to have the bells again recast and hung in an iron frame. The work was done by Taylor's bell foundry in Loughborough. This time the inscriptions were reproduced with new ones added. The treble and 2nd bells were recast with the words 'In memory of Edith Fanny Griffiths 1879–1950'. The 3rd bell acquired 'Recast by the Ringers: S. Daniels, L. Evans (Master). A. George, F. Harris, P. Hunt, P. Powles, E. R. Rock'. This 3rd bell had been made by Mears & Steinbank,

139

bell-founders of London, whose name was also reproduced together with those of the vicar, R. S. Aldridge, and the churchwardens of the time: P. L. Clowes, P. W. Turner 1906. This bell bore the motto: 'Fear God, Honour the King'.

The 5th bell had the addition: 'To commemorate the Coronation of Queen Elizabeth II 2. June, 1953'.

The 6th: 'In memory of Geo. Evans'.

The 7th: 'In memory of the Fallen 1914–18; 1939–45'. and 'P. E. Rock, Vicar'.

The tenor bell acquired the additional words: 'In memory of Ellen Vere Artindale'.

The work cost £1,500 4s. 0d.

Since a man had to be paid to ring the bell at customary times, the parish vestry, seeking to economise in 1838, resolved to discontinue the money for ringing the bell every Monday throughout the year and on 18 May, Oak Apple Day (Restoration of the Monarchy, 1660), 24 July and 5 November (Gunpowder Plot), as had been the custom.

In spite of this resolve, the bell-ringing must have continued, for the vestry had to order in 1843 'that the allowance for bell-ringing on 29th May and 5th November be discontinued', and in April 1851 'It was agreed that the custom of ringing the bell should be continued on the 24th May [Queen's Birthday], and 2s. 6d. allowed respectively to Messrs. Bassett and Macklin for refreshment to ringers'.

Chapter Thirty-Three

ECCLESIASTICAL HISTORY

Date	Vicar	Presented by
1278	Richard de Wyre, or Wye	Abbey of Lyre
1317	Walter de Mortimer	Abbey of Lyre
1335	Roger de Dene	Abbey of Lyre
1349	Richard de Gerneston	The King for Abbey of Lyre
—	Walter Grym	—
1403	John Snade	The Prior of St. Guthlac's
1476	Thomas Ellyott	Priory of Shene
14??	Thomas ap Richard, or Rhys	—
(fl. c.) 1501	Roger Whitehouse	—
1524	Miles Jeffys, or Jeffrey	Priory of Shene
1560	Thomas Lewis	Edward Langford
1594	John Birde	
1635	Richard Evans	
1663	Thomas Hollingworth	John Booth and Lucy, his wife
1669	William Bedford	John Booth
1726	Thomas Jones	Hon. Robert Price and John Dutton Colt
1771	Theophilus Lane	James Kinnersley of the Linch
1816	Frederick Rudge	Bishop of Hereford
1867	Joseph Barker	Bishop of Worcester
1902	Frederick William Worsey	Bishop of Worcester
1905	Richard Spencer Aldridge	Bishop of Birmingham
1917	Percival Alfred Hugh Birley	Bishop of Birmingham
1938	Percival Edward Rock	Bishop of Birmingham
1957	Harold Freer Harmer, L. Th.	Bishop of Birmingham
1962	Peter Nourse, R.D., M.A.	Bishop of Birmingham

The first vicar of Eardisland whose name is recorded is Richard de Wyre or Wye, who was instituted by Bishop Thomas de Cantilupe, later canonised as St. Thomas of

141

Hereford. That bishop's register reveals that the vicar was presented by the Abbey of Lyre in Normandy, which had probably been endowed with the Manor of Eardisland,* though in the Testa de Nevill of *c.* 1327 the Mortimer family then enjoyed the manorial rights. The manor belonged to William de Braos (d. 1211) but came to the Mortimers by Maud, one of his daughters. The arms of that family appeared in a north window of the church when Blount visited it in the reign of Charles II. There is a record that the Abbey of Lyre obtained leave to impropriate the rectory of Eardisland in the reign of Edward III (1327-1377) and created a vicarage. Walter de Mortimer succeeded Richard de Wyre in 1317 as rector, and it was probably he who initiated the considerable extensions which were made in about this period. As a Mortimer he, no doubt, had ample means. Was he the same Walter de Mortimer who was appointed to the rectory of Kingsland in 1315? If so, he may be the energetic builder of the church of St. Michael in that village, for Pevsner ascribes its building to the late 13th or early 14th century.

In 1326, the church of Eardisland was one of those in which one Richard de Staunton had to do public penance for killing a priest of Pembridge, Henry le Deyere. He is said to have been led to this act *instigante diobolo* but had secured absolution through the Pope's penitentiary, John de Wrotham. But he was obliged to perform a public act of penance in a number of churches. Besides Eardisland he had to appear as a penitent in the churches of Pembridge, Kington, Leominster, Almeley, Preston-on-Wye, and Shobdon. It would appear to have been very humiliating for the proud and impetuous baron.

In 1367 Bishop John de Trillek, when visiting the Deanery of Leominster, learnt that the poor vicar of Eardisland had very cramped quarters. He had no garden in which he could walk in solitude, or grow leeks and herbs, owing to the inadequacy of his endowment. The bishop therefore assigned to him a piece of land from the rectorial glebe.

*Lyre la Vielle, Eure, in the Canton de Rugles, which had property in Herefordshire, in 1086.

The monks of Lyre continued to present the vicars until, under Henry V, the alien religious houses lost their possessions in England. The rights of Lyre, in this respect, were transferred to the Carthusian Priory of Shene in Surrey which this same Henry founded in 1414. If, as is likely, the monks held the manor of Eardisland, that low tump with a flat top in the field called Monks' Court may have been the meeting place of the manorial court.

When the Priory of Shene was suppressed at the general dissolution of the monasteries under Henry VIII, the Manor of Eardisland came into lay hands. In the first year of Mary Tudor's reign, we read that 'the Rectory and Church of Eardisland were granted for 12 years to Edward Welch Esq.'.

In the 38th year of Elizabeth I, licence was given to Henry Vernon and his wife Ursula to alienate the Manors of Pembridge and Eardisland to Roger Vaughan, Esq., and his heirs. And again in Elizabeth's reign, date unknown, Eardisland Manor was granted by the Crown to Richard Barnard and Robert Tyler, yet in 1560 we find one Edward Langford presenting the vicar.

The Whittington family (*cf.* William, the founder of the grammar school) appear to have had the manor for a period in James I's reign for we learn that the manor was alienated by John Whittington, Esq. to another John Whittington, Esq. of Notgrove in 17 James I. Whether those who had the gift of the living were always the lords of the manor we do not know, but after a long period of lay patronage, the right of presentation came into the hands of bishops from 1816.

The places in Eardisland parish with the names 'Nun House' and 'Nunslands' lead many to think that there was once a convent of nuns in the parish. There is no evidence of this. The nuns referred to were probably the ladies of Limebrook Priory, 1.5km. south-east of Lingen (O.S. 375 661) who held property in the parish. In 1351 (Edward III) Adam Edgar bestowed his manor of Broxwood Power on the Prioress of Limebrook, to be held of the community, which was to keep his anniversary yearly. This Manor of Broxwood included the Nunslands and perhaps other lands adjacent. Another name for the Nunsland is 'Broxwood

Byrches'. Another property of the nuns was the Manor
of Marston, which came later into the hands of the
Monington family, as did the Riddox, near to the Nunslands.

There is a rather significant gap in the register between
1642 and 1657 which suggests that the incumbent left the
parish at the outbreak of the Civil War, and remained away
during it, and most of the Commonwealth period. There is
no evidence that, like so many of the orthodox Anglican
clergy, John Bird[1] was ejected in favour of a Presbyterian,
for such a minister would be expected to keep up the register.
During this period three entries of baptisms have been made
in English (unusual at that period) obviously at a later date.
One baptism is recorded for 1649, one for 1651, and a
third for 1653. When regular recording was resumed in
1657 two baptisms and three burials are noted. Only in
1658, two years before the Restoration, do we again find a
normal year.

The minutes or 'Journal' of the parish vestry, which have
proved such a fruitful source of later parish history, reveal
that the members were not always in tune with their vicars.
At the meeting of 26 December 1850, 'it was agreed by the
majority present that the Churchwardens should take legal
steps in respect of the recovery of a certain quantity of
Cloth, or the value thereof, from the Rev. Frederick Rudge,
the same having been taken from the Parish Church by him
or under his authority, it having been presented to the
Churchwardens for the benefit of the parish'.

Mr. Rudge appears to have been rather a Puritanical
clergyman and must have irritated a good number of his
parishioners. Under his chairmanship the vestry resolved
on 25 August 1825 'that the Churchwardens do immediately proceed to put into complete repair, the fences, gates
and roads belonging and leading to the parish church, as also
the Churchyard, and afterwards to take such measures as
are necessary to prevent all games of Fives, and every other
kind of sport, games or pastimes whatsoever in the Churchyard. Also that they have papers printed . . . absolutely
prohibiting any kind of Shows, pastimes, sports, games or

traffick of any kind during the Sabbath day, under the severest penalties which the Law can inflict'.

The Rev. Joseph Barker, who succeeded Mr. Rudge as vicar in 1867, seems to have been both an excellent and a deservedly popular man.

Shortly after his arrival in the parish he started the 'Eardisland Parish Magazine'. This continued to be published for nearly twenty years, and was sold at 2s. per annum. After 1881, when there were only 56 subscribers, it was sold at 2s. 6d. In 1888, the 'Leominster Deanery Magazine' was started in Mr. Barker's own home, and from that date Eardisland's notes were incorporated in that journal.

Mr. Barker was keen on proper doctrinal instruction. In 1871 his Lenten sermons were devoted to an examination of the Articles of the Creed. In the Lent of 1898 he started a children's service, which was well attended. He zealously prepared children for Confirmation, and the Confirmation of 1871 was held for the first time in living memory in Eardisland church. From the parish 15 boys and 16 girls were then confirmed; besides these, 12 children came from Pembridge, 11 from Kingsland and two from Bodenham.

Mr. Barker was a member of the Woolhope Club of Hereford, and contributed papers on local history in 1890 (a history of his own parish), in 1892, 1896 and 1901.

Shortly after his arrival in Eardisland, Mr. Barker bought the Staick House and made it his family home. He took a great interest in the work of the parish school, and encouraged parents to send their daughters there. The Rev. J. Barker was greatly assisted in his good work by his wife, who ran a Maternity Club to assist poor mothers. This kept a stock of sheets, neightdresses and layettes which could be borrowed by those in need.

FOOTNOTE

1. The Puritan Survey of 1642 reported: 'Vicaridge now vacant. Late vicar, Mr. Bird, an old man, noe preacher, nor in his youth of good life'.

Chapter Thirty-Four

RELIGIOUS DISSIDENCE

IT IS REGRETTABLE that no church registers and no churchwardens' minutes survive for the period immediately following the break with Rome, the formative years of the independent Church of England. The first register of baptisms, marriages and burials dates from 1614 and the first churchwardens' account from 1617. Had earlier records existed, we might have obtained some idea of the reactions of the parishioners to the drastic changes which took place in church worship between 1549 (the date of the first English Prayer Book of Edward VI) and 1570, when the Elizabethan Settlement was complete.

The Leen area was not without a fair number of 'popish recusants' in the late 16th and 17th centuries. The homes of a number of the gentry became the illicit centres for Catholic worship, and continued to give hope and encouragement to those who steadfastly . adhered to the old faith.

In 1620 Roger Vaughan of Kinnersley was lord of the manor of Eardisland, and the Vaughans of Kinnersley were notorious recusant Catholics. In 1641 Dame Jane Vaughan was indicted for harbouring the priest, Fr. John Broughton. Another family owning much land in the parish of Eardisland were the Moningtons, whose chief house was in the neighbouring Sarnesfield. The Moningtons kept the old faith alive in the area until Catholic emancipation came in the 19th century. One Monington house and estate in the parish was the Riddox. Marston Court in the adjacent parish of Pembridge, formerly the property of the nuns of Limebrook, was Monington property as late as 1870.

In 1624, Philip Froysell and the Crump family of the Porch House were presented as recusants, and for 'eatinge and drinkinge and feastinge with Catherine Kirwood, an excommunicate recusant'. Magdalen, Elizabeth and Mary Kirwood appear in a list of the recusants pardoned by James II in 1685. Mary Kirwood turns up again, together with Milborrow Deyos, widow, and her daughters, Mary and Anne and a Mrs. Berington, in 'A List of Papists in the County of Hereford', made pursuant to an order of the Privy Council in 1706, under Eardisland.

The Deyoses also seem to have been in trouble as Quakers, for the Bishop's Act Book of 1662 records that Nicholas Deyos and his wife were Quakers, that they paid no tythes or Easter Offerings, and kept private conventicles. William Kinnersley and his wife, also Quakers, keep private conventicles 'under pretence of preaching and praying'. In 1673 Nicholas 'Dyos' and his wife are again cited for their disobedience. They, along with Richard and Elianor Dolphin and their daughter, Sarah, are excommunicated for their repeated recusancy.

The names of two of the above recur in *A Collection of the Sufferings of the People called Quakers,* published in 1753.

'In the Month called July 1670, Nicholas Day (Dyos) of Eardsland, for a Meeting at his House, had eight Oxen taken worth 32 l.'.

In 1670 Richard Dolphin had four oxen taken from him worth 24 l, 'Which Oxen the Officers knew to be another Man's Property, yet regardless of Right, they took them'. Again, in 1676 'Taken from Richard Dolphin of Eardisland Cattle worth 48 l.'.

After the Revolution of 1688 the presentment of Protestant recusants was not required of the churchwardens, so that they were not prevented from worshipping where and as they liked. As those of Eardisland had no chapel, they probably helped to form the congregations of the various sects that flourished in Leominster.

A serious opposition to the Established Church was provided later by the Wesleyans, who built chapels in the village and at Barewood in 1864. The Eardisland chapel seated 150, and was well supported in the early years of this century. A stable was provided behind it for members who came in on horseback. Neither this chapel nor the one at Barewood ever had a resident minister. Both chapels were in the Leominster circuit, and were occasionally visited by its minister. Most of the services were conducted by lay preachers. The oversight of these chapels was later transferred to the minister of the Presteigne and Kington circuit. By 1955 the membership of the Eardisland chapel had shrunk to three.

Baptists in Eardisland

That there were Eardisland Baptists is revealed by a number of facts, but I have found no evidence that they ever had a proper chapel. The first young man of the Leominster Baptist congregation to enter the ministry was William Steadman of Eardisland. He entered the Bristol Academy in 1789. On completing his studies, he was ordained at Broughton, Hampshire. He held a co-pastorate at Plymouth and later became a tutor at Bradford College.

At the time of the Tithe Commutation one John West occupied property owned by the Baptist Society, represented by the Rev. Maurice Jones, who was the minister at Leominster from 1835–1846. The property was Plock Orchard and Tippets Brook House and garden. In a directory of 1863 a Baptist minister, the Rev. Samuel Blakesmore, is recorded as living in Eardisland.

Chapter Thirty-Six

SCHOOLS

NOTHING IS KNOWN of a school in Eardisland in medieval times, but it is possible, since the church had a chantry chapel, that its chaplain spent some of his time as a teacher as was usual. The chantry priests of Leominster and Kingsland were the schoolmasters there, so it may be that the school founded by William Whittington of Street was not without a predecessor. In his will of 1607 Whittington stated: 'I bequeath and give all that my portion of tithe in Street in the parish of Kingsland for and towards the erection and maintenance of a school within the parish of Eardisland, and the same to be erected, and the schoolmaster there to be continually elected by Roland Whittington and four others, and after their decease, the heirs of John Whittington of Horne shall have the election'.

The school house was shortly afterwards erected and a schoolmaster appointed. Why the people William Whittington mentions were unable to control the school's destiny we do not know, but we are surprised to find that as early as 6 July 1641 the Commissioners of Charitable Uses, while recording that the tithes and glebe lands with which the school had been endowed were worth at least £16 per annum, accused the rector of Kingsland, Dr. John Hughes, of collecting the said sum, and allowing the schoolmaster only £6 13s. 4d. for his maintenance. He had kept £4 per annum for his own use for upwards of seventeen years, to the prejudice of the school. Though he was ordered to pay it back he seems never to have done so.

In spite of this spoliation, the school appears to have continued to function right up to the time it was incorporated into the National School system c. 1821. The Bishop of Hereford licensed the schoolmaster who was usually a clergyman, capable of teaching Latin. The official school-master appears, at least sometimes, to have given the teaching to a deputy, for we learn that in 1821 the Rev. James Powell, M.A., was appointed master. He found the institution a mere sinecure as a grammar school, and appointed a deputy in order to conduct the school under the national system. He devoted the whole of his salary to the payment of his deputy, who in consequence received £39 per annum. For this salary he taught between seventy and a hundred children the three 'Rs'. At that date school hours were, in summer 8 a.m. to 12 noon, and 2 p.m. to 5 p.m.; in winter 9 a.m. to 12 noon, and 1 p.m. to 4 p.m. The children could start school at five years of age. In 1825 a new school was built by voluntary subscription on land given by the Rev. Canon Evans of Burton Court.

In order to cope with so many children of various ages, the master used the Madras system of education, so called because it was invented by one Andrew Bell, who was at one time the superintendent of the Male Orphan Asylum in Madras, India. It consisted in placing clever children, who had already mastered the elements, in charge of small groups to teach the less forward children the alphabet and so on.

Some schoolmasters must have had a very arduous life, for we find one, Henry Bullock, who in 1851 was also postmaster, parish clerk, grover and druggist. By 1859 he was assisted by a schoolmistress, Charlotte Williams.

In 1861 the parish vestry considered an offer of Mr. Evans of Burton Court to convey the School House to the parish. In reply, the members thanked him for the kind offer, but pointed out that the School House, having been built by public subscription and under the terms of the Street Court property, was already owned by the parish.

In 1872, the then owner of Burton Court, John Clowes, Esq., bought the old grammar school building and made it into a public reading room. In 1874 he bought the old schoolmaster's house and its site for £35. He gave a new site of equivalent area for a new schoolmaster's house and garden, close to the National School.

At first the pupils at the National School were probably all boys. In 1867 six girls were attending. Under the encouragement of the vicar, the Rev. J. Barker, the number of girls increased. (The Rev. Barker was the only licensed schoolmaster in the diocese of Hereford. The Whittington grammar school of which he was 'headmaster' had ceased to exist.) By 1870 there were 28 girls on the register; they were taught in a separate building.

As we have said above, the official schoolmaster, like the vicar, did not necessarily live in the parish or perform any duties there. In 1855 both vicar and schoolmaster lived outside the parish. This is the time when Henry Bullock was the poor hack who had to be so versatile in order to earn a living. One of his old scholars, writing his reminiscences for the admirable 'Women's Institute Book of Eardisland' of 1956 says that when he started school in 1857, Mr. Bullock was an old man. By that time some of the older boys would get the better of him. 'I well remember him chastising a boy named Parker, when two of the older brothers joined the younger in a scuffle with the poor old man. (Parker's was always a fighting family: Will died in a skirmish with natives somewhere abroad)'. In Bullock's time the lines of desks rose in tiers one above the other. 'The whole of the scholars in the writing lesson were plainly visible to our old chief, who for any little misconduct on our part used to spank us well on the head, or anywhere, with a long ruler which he used for the blackboard. Those who could write paid 3d. a month for pens and ink. Mr. Bullock made the quill pens we used, Wigmore Common supplying the needful goose-quills, which used to be gathered in that part by some of the scholars living there'.

The author of these notes had great respect for his new schoolmaster, Mr. Leigh, who, though a mere stripling, rapidly made great changes in the school.

A good deal of absenteeism resulted from the frequent floods, of which there were 84 between 1895 and 1950. For 45 of these the school had to be closed.

The school continued to take children aged from 5 to 14 until 1947. From then on children over 11 went to Kingsland for their secondary education; now they go to Weobley. In 1976 the school had 31 infants and juniors on roll, taught by the headmaster, Mr. Hope, assisted by Mrs. Chapel. In 1944, when the school was still taking children up to the age of 14 there were only 42 on the roll.

Since the 1870s some evening classes for adults have been held in the school from time to time.

The school was finally closed in 1979. By then the number of pupils had shrunk to seventeen.

Chapter Thirty-Six

SOCIAL HISTORY FROM PARISH VESTRY RECORDS

WE HAVE SEEN how the manorial court, the court leet, administered the property and regulated the agricultural operations of the villagers. Another aspect of their lives, their social well-being, was controlled by the parish vestry. The parishioners met annually at about Easter time to elect churchwardens and 'overseers of the poor' who were officers of the Poor Law. A note in their 'Journal' of 1830 explains: 'The inhabitants shall elect 5–20 inhabitant householder occupiers, and these are to be appointed under the hand and seal of one J.P.'. Eighteen were elected for Eardisland. The J.P. signing was John Taylor of Hardwick. The duties of churchwardens were manifold, as the following extracts from the 'Journal' will show.

The first mention of the churchwardens is dated 1617 when the vicar, John Birch, the churchwardens, Philip Froysell and William Griffiths, and three 'sidemen' agreed that whenever any of them should be called to Hereford to deliver 'presentment', or to do anything belonging to their office they should be allowed expenses.

The chief duty of the overseers was to care for the impotent poor, the aged, orphans and bastards. To relieve them, they were empowered to levy a 'lewn', or rate, to cover their expenses in paying weekly pensions, giving occasional alms or putting out children as apprentices. (Until the middle of the 17th century private charity amounted to a great deal more than official poor relief.)

The Elizabethan Poor Law which imposed this duty upon the churchwardens did not bear so heavily upon the ratepayers of the parish so long as recusants could be fined; a proportion of the fines was assigned for the relief of the poor. As the number of these declined, or as they were impoverished by the crippling fines, the income from this source diminished, and property owners were increasingly called upon to find more for the relief of the parish poor.

The vestry gets its name from the room in the church where its meetings were originally held, but, as the numbers attending grew, it was found convenient to hold meetings in private houses, inns, or the schoolroom. In 1749 it was held in the house of William Fencott. On this occasion the assembly considered the dangerous state of the steeple, and prepared a list of persons and places suitable for taking apprentices.

One of the least agreeable duties of the overseers was to discover the fathers of illegitimate children and make them pay, so that the parish would not be burdened. There were always a few of these, but at certain times the number grew alarmingly and the overseers acquired a special book in which to write names of children, mothers and fathers, which has the printed label 'Bastardy Book' (*c.* 1830).

As the parish was responsible for the maintenance of illegitimate children born within it, the officers tried hard to make sure that the children of non-parishioners were born outside the parish. Overseer's expenses: 'for going to Street with a girle that was big with Child and taking her away, 2s. 6d.' (1754). 'That Mr. Phillips, the Overseer, be authorised to instruct Mr. Woodhouse of Leominster to proceed against the Parish Officers of Dilwyn, or other Persons concerned in the illegal removal of Elizabeth Seaborne and her son from Dilwyn into this parish' (1834).

The following suggests a very harassed young woman: 'It was agreed that Mary Howells take her Bastard child Elizabeth to Mr. Weaver of Eaton, the father of the said Bastard, and if he refuse to take the said child, then the Bond which the said Mr. Weaver hath given to endemnify the Parish of Eardisland to be immediately put in suite, further that if the said Mary Howells doth Refuse to take her said Bastard, that her weekly pay be stopt till such times she hath complied as above' (1741). Later that year: 'Ordered that Mr. James Weavers's Bond for Indemnifying ye parish of Eardisland from the charge of his Bastard Child be immediately put in Sute'.

The overseers seem to have been fairly successful in extracting maintenance from fathers of illegitimate children. In 1832 they obtained £29 8s. 6d. from nine fathers for their children. Legal proceedings were taken against reluctant payers: 'That Thomas Ricketts of Pembridge be had before the Magistrates in order that he may be compelled to maintain his daughter now chargeable on the Parish, and repay the expenses already incurred' (1833).

Some fathers endeavoured to be discharged of further responsibility by offering a lump sum:

'Thomas Bodenham of the parish of Dilwyn having been taken into custody upon a charge of having gotten with child Ann Ricketts and having acknowledged the fact and offered £10 as an indemnity to the Parish for all costs and charges, it was considered insufficient. It is agreed that £15 be accepted as a full indemnity'.

The Parish Poor

The parish was responsible for the poor and unemployed but, though the overseers regarded it as part of their duty to be charitable to passers-by (as when they relieved a vagabond with 1s. in 1824, or three old soldiers 'that have a passport' with 1s. 6d. in 1827), they had to discourage penurious settlers from other parishes. In 1741 the vestry decided 'that the Overseers apply to a J.P. for a warrant, and bring all people that are not parishioners to swear their parish, and apply for an order to remove such people to their respective parishes . . . and also that application be made to a J.P. for the punishment of lewd women who brought any charge upon the parish'.

The deserving poor were at first maintained in their own homes by means of an allowance. In order to discourage the idle, in 1741 it was ordered that paupers should wear a placard showing that they were dependent upon the rates:

'ordered that all Popers that receive weekly pay as allsoe those that have their Rents paid, weare the Letters, and those that refuse soe to doe: 'tis ordered y^t ye officers stop their pay etc.'.

This device was resorted to again in 1834 when it was 'ordered that as a means of driving from the Workhouse all sound people able to maintain themselves, to affix upon some conspicuous part of their upper garments some badge or mark by which they will be known as paupers'.

The Workhouse

In 1575 the overseers applied to Lord Weymouth (Thomas, Lord of the Manor of Eardisland) for leave to enclose some land on the Bearwood and to build on it a workhouse. It was apparently refused.

In 1761 the 'Vestry agreed that Thomas Owen is to take a House for the Poor and to have the sum of £6 6s. for taking care of them for 1 year, and the Parish to allow him his Disbursements, and to give notice to Morrow to all Persons that of Parish rents Houses, that the paupers will leave the same at Chandelmas next'.

In 1762, they allowed £40 to a Mr. Preece for the 'maintenance, clothing and all other expenses that shall in any wise belong to the parish of Eardisland for the year only, the Parish to pay the Rent of the House and Barn, the rent being £3 13s. 6d. for the year. And he, the said Mr. Preece shall be at no expense in bringing nor taking of any person but within the parish'. Mr. Preece was succeeded by Mr. William Moore, who agreed to do the job for £39 for the year, the parish paying the rent. In 1775 the workhouse keeper, Thomas Ambler, was paid £65. In 1776 and 1777, John Miles was paid £60.

In 1781 it was felt necessary to take a firmer hand with the workhouse warden and to exercise more control over its running: 'At a Vestry Meeting this the 22nd Feb. 1781 it was agreed that Mr. Miles do continue to keep the poor for £60 till Candlemas next, Doctors or any Contagious Diseases excepted. It is also agreed upon and ordered that the Overseers of the Poor do at least once a week inspect the Workhouse and report to the Parish how the paupers therein are maintained in order that, if there be any just complaint, that the said Mr. Miles may be properly spoke to, and, if necessary farther dealt with, and he turned out, and the Workhouse let to another'.

At one time it was thought by some that the paupers in the workhouse could earn their keep, and efforts were made to keep them usefully occupied. Here are some examples of the work done and prices paid:

	s.	d.
Paid Henry Cole for weaving 22 yards of cloth at 3d. a yard	5	6
Paid Wm. Cole for weaving 32 yards	8	9
Paid Mary Edwards for spinning 2lbs. of Hurds ..		10
Paid Lyna Pember for boiling whitening and winding the yarn that Elizabeth Bowen spun	5	6

In 1830 the vestry records: 'In consequence of there being many persons burdensome to the Parish at this present time, and it being necessary to find employment for them, it is resolved that they shall be employed by the different occupiers of estates within the parish so long as is necessary'.

In 1832, 56 people were receiving weekly pensions for themselves or for children. An overseer appointed by the churchwardens was being paid £20 per annum. He had 11 women spinning, and paid rents of houses, including the workhouse, amounting to £27 2s. 9d., and spent £25 16s. 0d. on coal. His total disbursements amounted to about £355. In 1823-24 disbursements for the poor had been even higher at £476.

Some people in the workhouse tended to regard certain rooms as their own. One old lady housed members of her family there: '26. April 1832. Elizabeth Dubberley of the Workhouse is to remove from the room now occupied by her, her son and her daughter and to retire to a room assigned to her by the Overseers. Her son and daughter to provide situations for themselves—and her pay to be stopped from last Saturday, until sufficient proof is brought that Thomas

Dubberley is gone from her, and does not sleep in the same room with his mother and sister—upon which condition being complied with, the pay to be restored together with what has been stopped according to this order'.

In 1833 Elizabeth Dubberley was in trouble again. Her pay was to be stopped 'until she has got rid of the dogs she now keeps, and it shall appear certain that she keeps none at all, either upon her own or any other person's account'. In 1835 a Mary Hoskins was to have her pay stopped until she got rid of 'her very mischievous dog'. 'She does not need it.' Elizabeth Dubberley also again kept a dog and was threatened with loss of pay until she disposed of it. Long before, in 1822, the vestry had ordered that no person in the workhouse or receiving relief should keep a dog; the keeping of fowls by workhouse inmates was also forbidden.

In 1835 the parish officers took a hard line. On 12 March they decided that 'All fathers of Base Children' were 'to be pulled up and made to pay all arrears now due (without exception)', and on 26 March they 'resolved that due and proper notice be given to Mr. Smythies [who owned and let the workhouse] that they intend to give up the Workhouse at Candlemas next'. On 30 July of the same year they decided that 'notice be given to the different landlords receiving rents of this Parish or others who have their rents paid, that the same will be discontinued'. These stern measures were obviously found impossible to carry out to the letter, for in 1836 we find: 'John Smith and his wife— to remove from Hardwick to the Workhouse and to occupy the room now in possession of Elizabeth Pember, and Eliz. Pember to go into Susan Davis's appartment'. Even in 1840 the workhouse was still occupied, for Mr. Hudson, one of the Guardians, was authorised 'to allow one James Morton, *now in the Workhouse,* money not exceeding 6s. a week upon his quitting the same'. .The officers even helped 'Thomas Dubberley of Drury Lane with 10s. towards his arrears of rent'.

In 1844, 24 people had to be excused from paying rents because they were too poor.

Apprenticing Poor Children

In accordance with the 'Statute of Artificers' or 'Apprentices' of 1563, every child, unless exempt because its parents were propertied, had to learn a trade. For this he had to be apprenticed to a master for seven years, and the overseer had to arrange apprenticeships for the children in his care. A proper indenture was signed on these occasions, and in the parish chest is a sack of these indentures. The overseer was allowed one guinea to fit the child out in new clothes when he went to his master. Here are a few items of his expenses:

	£	s.	d.
9th Jan. 1823 . . . it was ordered that Mrs. Bull's daughter be bound apprentice to Mr. and Mrs. Haywood instead of his taking one of the next lot that are put out.			
17 March 1827. Paid for Bread, Cheese and Beer at Kingsland for the Children when they were put out apprentices:		3	6
12 April 1827. Allowed with each apprentice, 8 in number	8	8	0
Aug. 1830 to Betty Tippins going to Weobley to have her boy bound apprentice:		1	0
to clothe the apprentice:	1	0	0

One boy seems to have been specially favoured:

14 Aug. 1834 John Bowen to be apprenticed to Mr. Jones, Rope-maker of Leominster, if he is willing to take him for the £10 premium, and upon such conditions as are proposed.

Parish Medical Officer

The overseers paid for the medical care of the poor, and from at latest 1825 they were employing as a regular medical officer Dr. Charles Lomax of Weobley. In 1825 he was paid a salary of £10 10s. 0d. per annum; in 1831, £15.

Dr. Lomax agreed to attend not only the poor in the village, but the parish apprentices and paupers residing in the parishes of Weobley, Dilwyn, Kings Pyon, Pembridge, and Monkland.

In 1831 he contracted to attend the parish of Eardisland for three years, and agreed to resign if any negligence could

be proved. His contract included all cases of difficult midwifery and accidents, but excluded coroners' inquests and
hired servants.

At a vestry held on 2 July 1835 it was decided that 'the
Medical Officer should attend on a fixed day, chosen by
himself and at a place and time he finds convenient, so that
paupers, and the Overseer, can attend and state their
complaints'.

Dr. Lomax seems to have fallen from grace, for we find
this decision dated 14 January 1836: 'That Notice be given
to Mr. Lomax that the extra £5 allowed him will be discontinued or his Salary reduced to its original amount'.

When needed, Dr. Lomax had to be sent for from Weobley
and the parish officers claimed expenses for going on this
errand. To economise on this charge the vestry ordered in
February 1835 that this errand should in future be performed by a pauper on the pay-roll of the parish. 'In case
of such Pauper's refusal, all farther pay or relief to be
stopped'.

The Overseer of the Poor, and Constables

From the beginning of the 19th century the work of the
churchwardens as overseers of the poor had grown to such
an extent that they had to depute this part of their function
to a paid man. In 1819 the overseer, John Carpenter, who
had to pay regular weekly payments to 66 paupers claimed
£5 for 'serving the office'. In the year 1826–27 John Watkins
drew £10 for his labours.

In addition to his care for the poor, he had to pay for the
hire of rooms for vestry meetings, held usually at one of the
three public houses in the village, the *Bull,* the *Cross,* or the
Swan. He had to travel to other places on legal business;
he took the census and compiled the voters' list, and he
collected the 'lewn'. He paid the county rates; he paid for
summonses and warrants and for the services of the constables; for example: '1824. John Griffiths's Constables Bill:
£1 6s. 11d. John Tristham's Constables Bill: £1 1s. 6d.' He
paid for letters addressed to him as the Parish Overseer:

from Leominster, 3d.; Hereford, 5d.; from London, 11d. or 1s.

He paid the doctor, and he also paid for work done: in 1826 he paid the weaver for weaving 13 yards of cloth at 5s. a yard, and 16s. for four stone of hurds to be spun. He paid for cards and a wheel to employ some of the poor at 7s. 6d.

It is no wonder that after one year in office most of the overseers were glad to retire! They had to keep a careful account of their expenditure and submit their records to the inspection of the vestry at the end of their term of office. They often overspent and had to wait for their money until the next lewn was collected.

Some overseers were scarcely literate. James Tailor or Taylor who kept his accounts in 1831 had some significant spellings which probably reveal the contemporary local pronunciations: 'Wobble' for Weobley (*cf.* 'St. Weonards', pronounced Wonadz); 'Presteen' for Presteign; reeleef, warrand, Daves, Stremford (Streamford), whoman, meeten, shurt, jurny, jurne, shoose, 'puting Daveses wife two bed'.

Two 'petty' or parish constables were selected from a list of suitable men (aged 25–55) submitted by the vestry to a local J.P. Their office of 'keeping the peace' was not onerous, and they were only occasionally called upon, so that theirs was a part-time job for which they received a small payment. The vestry of 8 September 1842 was unanimous in believing that a salaried constable was totally unnecessary in the parish, and that two constables, one for the upper and one for the lower division of the parish, were sufficient to preserve the peace.

Parish constables were practically abolished by the County Police Acts of 1839 and 1840 which established the County Constabulary, yet up to 1894 constables and overseers were appointed in Eardisland.

The overseer occasionally took constables to arrest individuals who had offended, for example:

£ s. d.

20 Feb. 1826. Paid for a pint of Ale for Tristham
    when apprehending Charles Thomas: 3

£   s.   d.

21 Feb. 1826. Paid for Bread and Cheese, 1s. 7d. and
    Cider 2s. for Ann Davis, Sarah Leeke, John
    Preese, Charles Thomas and Tristham the Con-
    stable at Weobley: 3   7
    [Weobley had a lock-up]
26 Oct. 1831. Tristham, Constable for serving War-
    rants etc.   1   10   0
Yates, Constable for apprehending Corbet   5   0

    With some characters the overseer and the constables had
a busy time. The case of William Willett is a good example
of several.

£   s.   d.

12 Oct. 1824. Warrant and Complaint to take William
    Willett   2   0
2 Nov. 1824. Received Wm. Willett for his 2 children   2   0   0
2 Nov. 1824. Paid for Wm. Willett's commitment   ..   2   6
20 Nov. 1824. Paid Adams, Leominster, to redeem
    William Willett's bed   5   0
23 Dec. 1824. Mary Willett was receiving relief for
    her girl at the rate of 2s. p. week.
23 Dec. 1824. Paid Mr. Southal at the Cross for ale
    and Bed for William Willett   3   9
29 Dec. Paid for making a warrant at Ludlow te
    apprehend Wm. Willett   1   0
Paid Constable 2s. Spent 1s. with him at Ludlow   ..   3   0
Expenses of Bread, Cheese and Cider for Willett etc.
    at Ludlow and at the Maidenhead   4   9
Paid Horse Hire for Willett   12   0
Paid a Turnpike at Mortimer's Cross 1½
30 Dec. Paid for Bread and Cheese for Wm. Willett
    and Tristham at Kington 1s. 2d. Ale etc. 1s. 9d.   2   11
To keeping Willett and Tristham 2 nights, Breakfast
    and Supper and Breakfast on the 31st. Cider
    lodging incl.   4   0
Jan 8 Relieved Mary Willett by advice of Mr. Peoploe   2   0
Feb. 19. Paid for mending Willett's children's shoes
    by the advice of Mr. Taylor of Hardwick [a
    magistrate]   1   0
Mar 20. Paid Mr. Taylor of Hardwick for going once
    to Weobley and twice to Ludlow respecting
    Willett   7   6

    (In 1824 Mr. Lamb of Kington had paid £2 12s. 0d. for
Mary Willett's child. It is all very intriguing.)

Another case, that of Adam Yapp, serves to show how actively hostile parishes were to supporting people belonging to other parishes.

	s.	d.
Nov. 11, 1826. Relieved Adam Yapp's wife to have an order made	3	0
Nov. 12, 1826. Paid for Adam Yapp's Examination etc. when in Prison 1s. 6d.		
Copy of do.	1	6
Order to Removal 5s. and attendance at Gaol	8	0
To a journey to Hereford for an Order of Removal of Adam Yapp's family, his Examination etc. and a journey to Asshns hill [Aylestone Hill?] on the morrow to see James Preese, being obligated to stop in Hereford all night..	5	0
Nov. 17. Paid for Bread, Cheese and a pint of Ale at Leominster for Adam Yapp's wife		9
and a pint of Ale at the Laysters Pole for do. in removing her to the Laysters		3
A journey in removing Adam Yapp's family to the Laysters.		

Imprisonment for Debt

Early in the 19th century people were still imprisoned for debt. One parishioner seems to have evoked the sympathy of the vestry as the following 'Journal' entry shows:

Meeting at the *Cross*, 23 October 1823, the vestry decided, 'Mr. Thomas Caldicott of Lower Mill allowed expenses to go to Hereford to try to free from the County Gaol Mr. Baynham in prison for debt. He is to use his utmost endeavours to liberate him for the smallest sum which the parties concerned can be induced to accept, provided it shall not exceed £5'.

This was signed by the vicar, churchwardens and five others:

Some Unusual Overseers' Expenditures

		£	s.	d.
1752	a pair of Stays		3	0
1754	a pair of Stays for Hannah's Boy		2	6
1753	the Tack of a Bastard Child	1	6	0

		£	s.	d.
1751	3 stone of one-way Hemp			
	2 stone of one-way Thread..	1	3	0
	4 stone of Hurds	1	0	0
	paper Candles			11
	Handcuffs, one pair		3	0
1823	a Coffin for Posten's young one		7	0

Seven shillings appears to have been the normal price for a coffin, but in 1836 the coffin-maker must have offended the vestry seriously, for on 25 February the 'Journal' records:

'Edward Parker, having notoriously and shamefully violated his contract with the Parish relative to pauper coffins, ordered that he be desired to attend the next Vestry meeting and explain his conduct, and that in the meanwhile, in the event of any coffin being wanted for a pauper, the Churchwardens and Overseers do order the same to be made by anyone they please—and the contract now existing between him and the parish be terminated.'

Bad Money in the Rates, 1824–1831

Of the money collected in rates by the overseers during this period a surprising amount was regarded as bad, presumably forged.

1824	£248 contained £8.25 bad, i.e. ..	..	.. 3 per cent.
1825	£239 contained £3.6 bad, i.e.	..	.. 1.5 per cent.
1826	£242 contained £3.1 bad, i.e.	..	.. 1.3 per cent.
1827	£331 contained £4.5 bad, i.e.	..	.. 1.4 per cent.
1828	£240 contained £3.5 bad, i.e.	..	.. 1.5 per cent.
1830	£212 contained £2.25 bad, i.e. ..	..	1.1 per cent.
1831	£318 contained £3 bad, i.e.	..	.. 0.95 per cent.

Pestilence and Remedies

In 1831 and 1832 the fear of an outbreak of 'pestilence' in the district was very prevalent.

The churchwardens bought the first books of 'Prayers against Pestilence' on 10 December 1831 for 4s. From then on they bought books, costing 2s. 6d., on 18 February 1832,

9 March, 14 June, and 23 November. In December 1832 they spent one shilling on salt and vitriol to burn in the church, presumably in preparation for Christmas. 'For attending to the same' they were charged '9d. for Mon. ½ day'.

Survey of the Parish for Poor Rate Assessment

By 1827 so many ratepayers were dissatisfied by the way they were assessed for rates—on Land Tax valuation lines—that they met at the *Cross* inn on 16 November 1837 and decided to advertise in the *Hereford Journal* for a surveyor who would value and map and make an assessment for a 'Poor Rate'. At the *Bull* inn on 20 November 1837 a Mr. Sayce offered to map, value, measure and assess the parish at one shilling per acre. Feeling that this was overmuch they persuaded him 'to measure, value and estimate the Parish for 11d. per acre without a map, but providing a book of reference for the same'. They agreed to pay Mr. Sayce in two equal instalments, half on delivery and half three months later.

A month later they had changed their minds and demanded a map. The vestry agreed to raise a rate, not exceeding 9d. in the pound to pay for the survey and promised Mr. Sayce his extra one penny.

On 20 July 1838, Mr. Sayce supplied his new valuation and assessment, but no map. He demanded for his work £223 9s. 6d. to cover which a rate of 9d. in the pound at the new valuation would be required. He agreed to supply the map on receiving his second instalment.

It is clear from following events that many were dissatisfied with the new valuation. On 9 August various farmers in the parish sought contracts for haulage to cover part or the whole of their highway rates. Charges were laid down. Haulage was to be completed by 1 October. Furthermore, a note was sent to Mr. Sayce asking him to meet parishioners and explain some of his valuations.

At the *Swan* inn on 5 September 1839 the parishioners demanded that Mr. Sayce should complete his valuation by making an assessment on the tithes of the parish, considering that his valuation was incomplete while any rateable property remained unassessed.

Roads and Turnpikes

It seems that at this period there was a new emphasis on roads; better ones were demanded and this involved considerable expense. Naturally enough much opposition was provoked. A meeting at the *Bull* on 2 August 1828 decided what portion of the highway rate should be allotted for the use of the Kington Turnpike Trust. It was not to exceed £80, and it was to be entirely consumed within the parish and on hauling. One Job Juson was appointed by John Tong, the Surveyor of the Parish Highways, as collector of the highway rates.

From then on we hear of a series of wrangles as to the nature of the roads—whether they were 'team roads' or merely 'husbandry roads' or 'bridle roads'. Arguments as to whether one parish or the next was responsible for maintaining a road became common; Parish officers were authorised to summon   persons who refused to pay their rates, 'so as to compel them'.

Soon, in 1844, it had to be admitted that some people were too poor to pay rates, and 24 parishioners and six non-parishioners (though residents) were excused.

The lord of the manor, the Rev. J. R. Smythies, and the vicar, the Rev. Frederick Rudge, owners of tithes, were obviously reluctant to pay the rates for which they were assessed. On 21 May 1846 the vestry resolved that Mr. Baker, the overseer, should call and demand the rate due from Rev. J. R. Smythies, of the Linch, granted 4 February 1846, 'and in case of refusal, he is authorized to call on Messrs. Miles and Sale for instructions to obtain it'.

On 28 May 1846 it was agreed to rate Mr. Smythies at 6d. in the pound on £504 10s. 3d., and Mr. Rudge at 6d. in the pound on £303 14s. 2½d.

In February 1847, 27 people had to be excused from paying rates; in April the number had risen to thirty-five.

In 1848 the churchwardens were instructed to give notice to the parishes of Pembridge and Staunton, and to the clerk of the peace, that the parish of Eardisland was withdrawing from the Union of Roads with these parishes.

In the same year the vestry agreed that henceforth the overseers should apply to the Receiver of Vicarial Tithes for all rates, as soon as they were assessed, and, if denied, apply to the magistrates to recover them.

By this time the Turnpike Trusts were undertaking the repair and maintenance of the roads, but the tolls they charged in this area were not enough for them. In 1840 the surveyor of the Kington Turnpike Trust appealed for aid towards the Turnpike road in the parish. The overseers regarded £70 as an adequate contribution.

As an example of the sort of problem with which the vestry was confronted the following is typical. Because of the number of parishioners interested, the meeting was held in the schoolroom on 28 March 1850. The road from the Broom to Clearbrook had long been a bone of contention. The vestry proposed to suspend work on the road until a vote could be taken. 'It was proposed that the road called Folly Lane leading from Eardisland Bridge over the Arrow to that part of a certain Bridle way heretofore part of a certain way called Bagley Lane in this parish of Eardisland to Clearbrook in the parish of Pembridge shall be recognised and maintained as a Bridle road only. The survey is to oppose any attempt to burden this parish with the expense of maintaining such roads otherwise'.

Two polls were held. Altogether 166 voted and a majority of 78 was against maintaining Folly Lane as a team road.

In connection with this vote it is interesting to observe the high proportion of illiteracy in 1850. Fifty-four (i.e., 30 per cent.) of the voters could not sign their names.

This was not the last of the matter, for at the Spring Assizes of 1853 the parish was indicted 'for not repairing a certain alleged Highway leading from Clearbrook by Twyford to the Broom'. This was 1,400 yards of road eight yards wide. The vestry of 28 July 1853 decided that the indictment should be defended. Messrs. Banks and Son, solicitors of

Kington were to be instructed to conduct the inhabitants' defence.

The Sayce Valuation of 1838 called into Question

The rates continued to be felt an intolerable burden by the landlords. On 19 June 1851, the Rev. J. R. Smythies proposed that in the opinion of the meeting the present 'Valuation and Assessment for the relief of the Poor', as made by Mr. Sayce, was, when made, a fair, equal and full account of the rateable property in the parish, but from the permanent depression in agricultural produce it now greatly exceeded the actual value. The meeting agreed, after discussion, to reduce the valuation made by Mr. Sayce by one fourth, and decided that all future rates should be made at that reduction.

In 1851 Mr. Smythies was active again in defence of his property. On 21 August he obtained the vestry's consent to this resolution: 'The portion of Long Meadow for which Mr. Smythies, as he states, is overcharged to Eardisland, should be given up to Pembridge parish in lieu of a part of Wesley, which was given up to Eardisland in deciding the Boundary line'.

On 22 February 1855 Mr. John Macklin proposed that the rates should be returned to the original value made by Mr. Sayce.

In about 1880 there was further agricultural depression, and another list of persons from whom it was impossible to demand rates was approved. People again appealed against the rates as fixed. Alterations were approved in 1883. In 1886 and 1887 meetings were held to examine the Valuation list and make further alterations.

The Railway as a Source of Rates

When the railway from Leominster to Kington had to pass through the outskirts of the parish a new opportunity to obtain a relief to the rate burden was visualised, and in August 1858 the surveyor was directed to have measured the land in the parish through which it passed. He was then to 'make application to the Company to ascertain what amount of rate they were willing to pay'.

Belated Appreciation of Turnpike Roads

Alas! the railway spelt the ruin of the Turnpike Trusts, and now that their end was near, the parishioners of Eardisland began to appreciate them. When the vestry, in 1866, received a letter from the Secretary of State requesting the opinion of the parishioners as to doing away with the Turnpike Gates on the Leominster Trust, the meeting was unanimous in its opinion that the Turnpike Tolls should not be abolished!

Chapter Thirty-Seven

OCCUPATIONS

AS LONG AS IT HAS existed, Eardisland has been no more than a village in an area of fertile land, so it has never developed anything we should now call an industry. In the past it depended upon Leominster, the metropolis of the area, for the products of medium-scale industry. Nevertheless, certain specialised trades useful to an agricultural population have been practised in the past. Until quite recent times smiths and builders have managed to make a living in the neighbourhood.

For seven years, 1699–1706, the vicar, then William Bedford, included in his Latin register the names of his parishioners, and their status or profession. For example, William Brewster, as Lord of the Manor of Burton, is styled *generosus* (a gentleman); John Lewis is an *operarius* (a labourer); trades included *tector* (thatcher), *sutor* (shoemaker), *faber* (smith), *opifex* (artisan), *piscator* (fisherman), *molendinator* and *molendinarius* (both miller), *fabricator* (builder), *calciarius* (lime burner), *textor* (weaver), and *chirothecarius* (glove-maker); the term 'yeoman' is not translated.

There must have been 'colliers' or charcoal burners working in the 26 acres of woodland on the Hinton Manor estate, which were represented on the tithe map by the field names 'Coalworks Piece' and 'Coal Tree Field'. One wonders if these were the colliers who are said to have helped cause a riot outside the gaol in Hereford in 1775, when some of their friends from the country tried to rescue the men who had attacked Arrow Mill, Kingsland. It may be that much of this charcoal was used in the smelting of iron at Strangworth Forge in the parish of Pembridge. The charcoal-producing area, adjacent to what is now the Broome farm and near Lady Pools (the source of the River Pinsley) may have been called 'Tree Brome', for in an old MS. of *c.* 1675, we find among the villages of the parish of Pembridge, Leen, Milton, Noke, Twiford, Tree Brome and Strangwoods.

The above-mentioned millers were probably those of Upper and Lower (Glan Arrow) mills, or Burton Mill, all of which were water-mills, but at some time there was probably also a windmill, for we find the name 'Windmill Coppice' in Burton. The water-mill in the centre of the village was grinding corn up to 1950.

Of course there were always innkeepers, but one suspects that they, like the schoolmaster, had other part-time jobs. Carpenters, wheelwrights, coopers, basket-makers and tailors have flourished in small numbers, and tanners left their name in the Tanhouse; all these trades had representatives in Eardisland until 1851. Most of the villagers, however, worked as labourers or in other capacities as servants of the wealthier farmers. In 1856, 13 people described themselves as 'farmers'. By 1895 the number had risen to 36, and by 1941 it had fallen to twenty-seven. But from 1876 onwards people calling themselves 'smallholders' have grown in number. From three in 1895 the number grew to 16 in 1937, and was still 14 in 1941.

Labourers and servants in the pre-industrial era were hired for one year at the fairs of Leominster and Pembridge. It is said that as many as two hundred farmers sometimes appeared at the Pembridge fair to hire their servants. The men seeking work stood in a group in the market place, each wearing something to indicate the sort of work he was capable of doing. A shepherd wore a wisp of wool in his slouch hat, a waggoner wore horse-hair, and so on. The farmer hiring a man gave him a shilling to clinch the deal. Once hired, the man took the sign of his trade from his hat and proceeded to enjoy the fun of the fair with his shilling.

The women wore no sign of their speciality. They were distinguishable from the mere spectators of the show only by being more soberly dressed. They remained standing aloof from the gay crowd until they were hired. If a farmer's wife liked the appearance of a girl, she would walk all round her, examining her as carefully as a dealer would examine a horse he thought of buying. If she was satisfied, she would ask, 'Do you want a place?' If the girl replied, 'Yes, Ma'am', the mistress questioned her further. 'Where have you lived? What can you do?', etc. If the answers satisfied the mistress, she hired the girl by giving her a shilling. Once a servant had commenced in his new place, he was bound for a year. The Pembridge hiring fair lasted until about 1900.

In these days of the motor car, the variety of professions pursued by the inhabitants must be greater, for many work in Leominster and Hereford. A fair proportion of the present inhabitants are retired people seeking the quiet of rural life after a life of activity in big cities.

A Peripatetic Miller

According to a well-known German song 'to wander is the miller's joy', and this appears to be borne out by the story of one miller in our area. It was told me by his daughter, Mrs. Harris, who now lives in Leominster. This miller, a Mr. Davies, operated in turn the following water-mills:

1. New Mills, Dilwyn, where my informant, Mrs. Harris, was born,
2. Knightwick Mill, Worcestershire.
3. Goodrich Mill.
4. Beulah Mill, Breconshire.
5. Nantmel Mill, Radnorshire.
6. Wegnals Mill, near Rodd and Presteigne (this was situated on a track, a traditional route to Kington, much frequented by tramps).
7. Staunton-on-Arrow Mill.
8. Mortimer's Cross Mill, supplying flour up to 1933.
9. Aymestrey Mill.

His wife used to obtain bolting cloth of various finenesses from Switzerland. With this she made sieves to fit the mills. She was herself the daughter of a miller, Mrs. Cornes of

Forge Mill, Pembridge, then a flour mill. Although working as a teacher, her daughter helped to operate the mill. Mrs. Cornes was also associated with the mill at Coed Henry where she was born.

Millers often paid their rents in 'sticks' of eels, which were trapped in a special device at the mill, and speared out when their wriggling masses were dense enough (a stick consisted of 25 eels).

Wages of Farm Labourers and Craftsmen

In 1808 the wage of a farm labourer was 7s. a week, and with this he kept a wife and family. No doubt he earned extra at harvest time. At the period of the prices of commodities listed below he cannot have earned much more, for his wage in 1855 was 9s. a week, and 1858 and 1860 only 8s. per week. From 1864 it continued gradually to rise so that after 1890 it fluctuated between 12s. and 14s. The Great War brought about a considerable rise, for by 1916 it was 25s. a week, and by the end of the war it had risen to 45s. Then occurred the slump, so that the labourer's wages fell to 27s. a week by 1926. Even in 1935 his wage was only 35s. per week. The second World War made his work valuable so that he drew from 41s. 6d. to 54s. In 1955 his wage was 127s. a week, and in 1976 £42-46.

Craftsmen, of course, could demand higher wages. In 1873 a skilled tiler earned 3s. a day; in 1875 a timber-feller earned from 12s. 6d. to £1 a week; and in 1880 a master wheelwright earned 4s. a day.

Cost of Commodities 1825–1830

(derived from churchwardens' accounts)

	£	s.	d.
Frock, i.e., a Smock, for a boy		9	0
Smock frock and shirt for an Apprentice		3	0
To clothe an Apprentice	1	1	0
Jacket and Waistcoat		7	8
Petticoat		2	0
Shift		1	0
Pair of Shoes		6	3
ditto		4	0

Cost of Commodities—*continued*

	£	s.	d.
Pair of Small Clothes		4	4
Flannel for Breeches		4	3
1 yard Flannel		1	0
2 yards Flannel		1	8
Sheeting, per yard			7½
50 yards Calico		18	0
Sheeting 5 yds. at 7½d. per yd.		3	1½
Cloth per yard: 6d. and 7½d.			
2 stone one-way Thread	1	3	0
1 stone hurden Thread		9	6
4 stone Hurds	1	0	0
3 lbs. Hurds at 5d. per lb.		1	3
4 coffins and shrouds	3	8	0
1 lb. Mould Candles			6
Paper Candles? (number not given)			11
1 peck flour		2	6
Flour ½ bushell		6	0
,, ,, ,, (next year)		4	6
Mutton, per lb.			5
Coal, per ton		16	0
Handcuffs, per pair		3	0
800 bricks (for Workhouse)	1	6	0
Cost of Printing Voters' List 1832		10	0
Wool 2 lbs. (1824)		2	8
3 days work, taking the Population		10	0

Prices *c.* 1830 compared with those of 1976

	c. 1830	1976
	£	£
A pair of leather shoes	0.25	10-12
¼ bushel of flour	0.30	1.70
1 lb. mutton	0.02	0.80
1 ton coal	0.80	37.50
A petticoat	0.10	3.00
A coffin	0.73	40.00
1,000 bricks	1.63	30.00

Chapter Thirty-Eight

LANDOWNERS AND TENANTS

OF THE THREE MANORS contained in the ecclesiastical parish of Eardisland, the chief, that of Eardisland itself, was the property of monks up to the Dissolution of the Monasteries, when it fell into lay hands. Hinton and Burton had lay owners from the 14th century at latest. A bailiff of the Manor of Kingsland mentions Hinton as his lord's property in 1390. There were lords of the manor of Hinton until *c.* 1930, when John Paton of Waun Wern, near Pontypool, Co. Monmouth, was the last claiming this title. Burton's first lord of the manor was Ralph de St. Owen in 1332 and we have an almost complete list of its masters from then until the estate was broken up and sold in 1949.

These owners of great estates did not always live on their estates, the management of which was left to stewards or bailiffs. The various farms which constituted the manor were let out to tenants and the lord lived from the rents.

We have a list of the owners of estates in Eardisland, compiled in 1637:

> Thomas Walle Gent. was the owner of Eardisland's demesnes.
> Peter Smith gent. owned Hinton's demesnes.
> John Cotes (or Coates) owned the manor of Burton.

Other freeholders were the following:

Owner	Property
Henry Hyet, gent.	Twiford
Robert Lotchard, gent.	a living at Hinton
John Deyos, gent.	Nun House
William Smallman, esq.	a living in Eardisland
Nicholas Kyrwoode	a living in Eardisland

175

Other freeholders—*continued*

Owner	Property
Isacke Weaver, gent.	a living in Eardisland
Henry Taylor	a living in Eardisland
John Parker	a living in Hardwick
John Crofte, gent.	the lower farm in Burton
James Munne, gent.	a living in Burton
Richard Morris	2 houses and land in Burton
John Stalward	a living in Hardwick
Thomas Colcumbe	a living in Barewood
Hugh Rosse	a house and land at the Barrowe
Richard Monington, esq.	a living at the Riducks
John Bowier, gent.	a living at Broxhill
Walter Crumpe, gent.	a living at the Birches
Richard Anwell, gent.	the Nun Lande

At the period of the 'Act for Inclosing lands in the Parish of Eardisland' of 1811 the chief landowners were John Robert Smythies, Marianne Atherton and Charles Haywood.

In 1863 the chief property-owners were John Harding, Esq. (who was also Lord of the Manor of Eardisland), Lord Bateman, and the Rev. William Edward Evans (Lord of the Manor of Burton).

In 1870 they were John Harding (no longer described as lord of the manor), Benjamin Lawrence Sanders, John Clowes (Lords of the Manors of Hinton and Burton respectively) and Lord Bateman.

In 1891 the situation was as in 1870 except that John Harding had died and his trustees had replaced him.

In 1909 the chief landowners were: Lt.-Col. Peter L. Clowes of Burton Court; John Paton of Waun Wern, near Pontypool, Mon. (who was then Lord of the Manor of Hinton); Lord Bateman of Shobdon Court; Mrs. Peake; Lacon Lambe of Dilwyn; William Charles Haywood, and Mr. John Price.

In 1926 P. L. Clowes of Burton, John Paton, Mrs. Burton, and Messrs. C. H. Tinsley, Henry Gittins, Thomas Lewis and the Messrs. Norman and Brian Tebb were the chief landowners.

Now the three manors have been broken up, the land is owned by the farmers who cultivate it, or let it 'on tack' to other farmers.

The farming practised is generally mixed, as it always has been. A fair amount of grain has always been cultivated. Cattle, especially pedigree Herefords, have been bred and sold for meat, and sheep and pigs are commonly kept. Flax used to be grown in the low-lying fields near the source of the Pinsley. Hops were once grown to a considerable extent, but are now scarcely to be seen in the parish. Beans and roots are grown, and several market-gardens are run by small-holders. Lynch Court specialises in high quality fruit, most of which is bought by Marks and Spencers.

Owing to the use of machinery, the number of farm-labourers employed has continued to fall. For fruit-picking most of the labour is seasonal and women and children, largely recruited from Leominster and transported by the growers, earn extra cash at harvest times in this way.

As the cost of labour adds so much to the price of fruit, many growers invite customers to pick their own, and of late this method of selling has proved very popular.

Known Lords of the Manors in the Parish

Eardisland

1211. William de Braos.

c. 1327. Members of the Mortimer family.

Prior to the Dissolution of the Monasteries this manor appears to have been the property of religious houses: Lyre in Normandy first, and later Sheen in Surrey.

1620. Roger Vaughan of Kinnersley.

1637. Thomas Walle, gent.

1663–9. John Booth.

c. 1726. Robert Price and John Dutton Colt.

c. 1772. James Kinnersley.

c. 1790. Thomas, Marquis of Bath, Viscount Weymouth.

1851, 1858. James Kinnersley Smythies.

c. 1863 John Harding, Esq.

1891. Trustees of the late John Harding.

Hinton

    1637. Peter Smith, gent.
    c. 1715. Robert Cutler.
    c. 1734. Bryan Crowther.
    c. 1870–1900. Benjamin Lawrence Sanders of Street.
    1909–1926. John Paton of Waun Wern, near Pontypool.

Burton

    1332. Ralph de St. Owen.
    1356. A Lady of the Manor.
    1376. A Lady of the Manor.
    1384. A Lady of the Manor.
    1399. Another Ralph de St. Owen.
    1402. Thomas Seyntowen.
    1403. Patrick Seyntowen.
    1422. Roger Atkin was seneshal.
    1428. Thomas and Margaret Downton.
    1492. John Blount armiger was seneshal.
    1505. John Cotys (or Cotes).
    1527. In trust for John Cotys' widow and their son.
    1554. John Cotys.
    1562. John Cotes.
    1637. John Coates, Esq.
    1673. John Brewster.
    c. 1726. A member of the Croft family of Croft Castle.
    c. 1745. John Brewster.
    c. 1851–63. Rev. William Edward Evans.
    1863–70. John Clowes.
    1900–49. Lt.-Col. Peter Legh Clowes, and after his death,
              Mrs. Clowes.

Chapter Thirty-Nine

POPULATION

THE POPULATION of the parish seems never to have reached a thousand. We have no records of the total population before 1831, but a study of the number of baptisms in the church register gives the impression that this remained fairly stable between 1614 and 1770, for during this period the annual average was about eleven. The number shot up to 20 in 1780, and from this time until 1880 the average was 21 per annum. From then on the number has steadily fallen. In 1970 the figure was one.

Census Returns

Year	Ecclesiastical Parish	Civil Parish
1831	791	Not known
1851	899	,,
1861	894	,,
1871	886	,,
1881	781	,,
1891	684	500
1901	679	470
1911	649	508
1921	643	496
1931	596	437
1941		
1951	597	463
1961		474
1971		439

Year	Baptisms	Funerals	Marriages	Totals of all three
1614	6	19	1	26
1615	10	13	3	26
1616	9	18	4	31
1617	12	12	—	24
1642	14	11	0	25
1658	10	9	4	23
1660	12	5	1	18
1662	7	7	2	16
1673	8	3	1	12
1676	10	8	1	19
1681	13	7	3	23
1685	17	10	4	31
1688	7	11	3	21
1694	9	11	1	21
1701	14	5	2	21
1709	15	9	1	25
1712	14	12	2	18
1726	13	11	2	26
1730	10	9	6	25
1740	13	16	4	33
1750	17	7	1	25
1760	9	7	0	16
1770	7	5	0	12
1780	20	21	5	46
1790	30	16	3	49
1800	16	10	6	32
1810	31	11	4	46
1813	20	12	1	33
1820	18	15	1	34
1830	23	19	6	48
1840	15	16	2	33
1850	18	22	2	42
1860	30	12	4	46
1870	18	14	1	33
1880	20	24	5	49
1890	17	9	4	30
1900	10	8	4	22
1910	9	10	0	19
1920	9	7	2	18
1930	10	9	2	21
1940	7	8	3	18
1950	7	3	0	10
1960	5	2	4	11
1970	1	0	2	3

Longevity in Eardisland Inhabitants

When studying his parish registers, the Rev. Joseph Barker, the vicar in 1890, noticed that an unusually large number of the inhabitants died at an advanced age. He reported that since 1778, 112 years before, no fewer than 38 had reached the age of 90 and upwards. Twelve died at 90, three at 91, seven at 92, one at 93, two at 95, two at 96, five at 97, two at 98, one at 103, and one at 108. One, Elizabeth Perry, died in 1819 at the age of 108 at Streamford, within 200 yards of her birthplace at Shirlheath. The *Hereford Journal* of 9 June 1819, has this report of this remarkable old lady:

> Her sight was a little impaired, but she could eat and drink and take snuff, of which she was very fond. To the last she could walk in and about the house, with the assistance of her daughter. She had enjoyed uninterrupted good health and her death was the result of age, as she kept her bed only on the day previous, and retained her faculties to the last. She attributed her protracted life to hard work and hard living.

Her eldest daughter was at this date 84, and her younger son sixty. She remembered 'Muncorn' (sometimes called monk-corn, as it was made in the Middle Ages by monks)— a mixture of wheat and rye—selling at 6d. a bushel, and butter at 2d. per pound.

Chapter Forty

CHARITIES

IN ADDITION to the Whittington Grammar School which has been dealt with previously, Eardisland had four more bequests for the relief of its poor.

The oldest is what has come to be called the 'Court House Charity' because it is paid out of the Court House estate.

An ancient document records that a certain, unnamed, lord of the manor of Eardisland gave the 'tenth' in the several parcels of land, formerly arable, which are named as follows: the New Tidings, four acres, in which were six ridges. In Sheepcote Furlong and Lime Gobbett, 20 acres in which were 20 ridges. In Shurlefield, four gobbets or parcels of land, between Greenclose and the Nunhouse Acre at Fowleslough, called But Furlong, in which the tenth ridge was due. In Streame Field, half a tenth ridge. In Quarry Furlong, 10 acres, in which were 10 ridges. In West Field Gobbett, 20 acres, in which were 20 ridges. In Denshall Field, 15 acres, in which were 15 ridges. In Church Field, 14 acres in which were 14 ridges. In Smely, 30 acres in which were 30 ridges.

These tenth ridges were given by the lord of the manor to the person of the said parish who should be his farmer or deputy there, being for the maintenance of a perpetual alms; and that he should in lieu thereof, distribute to the poor of the said parish of Eardisland most wanting, 13 bushels of wheat and 13 pence in silver to 13 boys of the said parish, for a remembrance of that gift.

The document further states that most of the said parcels of land had been converted intó pastureland (evidence of enclosure before 1670), and that the said alms would have

182

been lost if John Booth, Esq., the then farmer of the said parsonage of Eardisland, had not commenced a suit against Mr. Richard Dolphin, who would have defrauded the poor of their alms.

The above suit was commenced *c.* 1670, as the evidence of a certain witness was taken on 19 October of that year, and confirms some of the above facts.

No documents are available, but the above charges are paid out of the Court House Estate to the parish officers and distributed by them on the Thursday before Easter; the wheat to the poor in general, in quantities from half a quarter to a peck, according to the number in family, having regard to merit, and the 13 pence to the children.

(This is extracted from the printed reports of the former Commissioners Enquiring Concerning Charities, No. 32, Part II, 30 June 1837. In this year the overseers hired a room at the *Cross* inn for the use of the Charity Commissioners.)

Froysell's Charity

In 1730 Alexander Froysell left a sum of money, the interest on which was to be used for the poor. When the Commissioners reported in 1837 this interest amounted to £1 13s. 5d. per annum.

At a parish meeting in April 1743 we read: '. . . 'tis agreed that the money left for the use of the Poor of this Parish by Mr. Alexander Frazol deceased be forthwith put to interest to Mr. John Smyth of Eardisland upon Security approved by Mr. John Brewster, and the lawful interest be laid out and distributed in Bread by the approbation of the Resident Minister, Churchwardens and four of the Inhabitants of this parish as Mr. Frazol's will directs, i.e. to be distributed to the poor in Bread upon Candlemas Day every year. We at this meeting think it convenient that Mr. Smyth (as is by him proper) settle for the Security of this Legacy the Sitches [*sic*] Estate and we do nominate and appoint Trustees Bryan Crowther and John Lambe. We agree that the aforesaid John Smyth be at no charge for the Writings. (Eleven members signed.)

In 1837 the bread was distributed and paid for by Marlowe's Charity.

Marlowe's Charity

In 1773 Miss Mary Marlowe of Leominster, a rich and charitable Baptist, made a number of bequests for various good purposes in Leominster and its surrounding villages. To the poor of Eardisland she left 13s. 10d. per annum to be expended in threepenny loaves.

Leinthall's Charity

In the 18th century the old Herefordshire family of Lenthall, Leinthill or Leinthall still had its kindred living as lesser gentry at Hardwick in Eardisland. Leinthalls served as churchwardens in 1715 and 1736. One of them, probably Thomas, left £1 4s. 0d. per annum, derived from a cottage and garden, for the poor. In 1794 this was vested in Thomas Howard, and like the other charitable income, it was distributed in bread.

Gleaning

An unchartered charity was the right of the farm-labourer's wife to gather any heads of corn left lying about the fields after the harvest. She would feed the barley to the pigs and have the wheat ground at the local mill. One poor woman, the mother of seven children, is said to have gleaned so industriously that she collected enough wheat to feed her family for six months of the year. The farmer allowed her to buy what she needed for the remaining six months at the rate of threepence a week.

Chapter Forty-One

EARDISLAND PLACES AND NAMES

WHEN MEANINGS are given it must be understood that these are speculative. A few names are self-explanatory.

Arrow, River; 'Arewe' 1256. A British river-name cognate with Welsh *ariant,* 'silver', etc.

Bannut Tree Fields and Walk: 'bannut' = walnut (on Hardwick estate).

Barewood, Bearwood: both forms in use. If 'Bear' is from O.E. *bearu,* 'wood', the name is tantologous. Bannister suggests 'barrow-wood', as there is a barrow within half a mile.

Barrow: in general, this very common name represents the Old English *bearu,* with dative form *bearwe,* 'grove, wood'.

Birches: probably from a clump of birch trees.

Black Hales or Harls: the plural of Old English *halh,* 'a corner'. 'Hales' usually suggests a remote valley.

Brockaly: first element may represent Old English *broce,* 'badger', or Old English *broc,* 'brook', and *ley,* 'wood, glade'.

Broom: the shrub which was once abundant here.

Brouch, The: probably refers to the brook (Southall's brook) which traverses the farm.

Broxhill: brock, 'badger' (*cf.* Broxwood).

Coal Tree, Coal Works, Fields: it appears that these fields were once covered with woods in which charcoal burners, 'colliers', were active.

Court House: the house in which the manorial court was held at one time.

Dowsage: black sedge.

Duppas Land: land with which Bishop Duppa endowed his Pembridge almshouses.

Flax Piece: near the river Pinsley where flax was formerly grown.

Friths, The: Old English (ge-) *fyrhd,* 'wood'. Coppice or woodland.

Gailess Farm: Gailess possibly a personal name.

Gallifers Means: a proper name in conjunction with *means,* 'property, wealth'. An MS. records that 'William Golafer was possessed of lands in Pembridge manor and gave part of them to the Priory of Wormsley'. Gulliver is another form of Golafer.

Gaul Ditch.

Glan Arrow: (mill).

Hardwick: herd plus *wick,* 'farm'.

Hinton: hean-tun—'high tun'.

Knapp House: Knapp Orchard.

Lady Pool: the brook that once flowed under the Priory House in Leominster rose here. 'Our Lady's pool.'

Legions Cross: this is reputedly the Saxon name of this crossroads.

Lymes, The: possibly from a clump of lime trees once growing there (not lime quarries).

Lynch, The: Old English *hlinc,* 'ridge, bank, balk of land', any bank or boundary. It is not far from the Rowes Ditch.

Medless: 'unruly', 'unrewarding'.

Merry Prill: prill, 'a small stream of water'.

Monks Court: place where the court leet was held in the days when the monks were lords of the manor.

Nut Field (a farm): perhaps another place where 'bannut' (walnut) trees were cultivated.

Orls, The: 'alders'.

Pigmoor: a common.

Porch House: this is now called Manor House; 'Porch' because this feature was conspicuous.

Riddimore: a descriptive word, 'ruddy', plus 'moor'.

Riddox: Redox, Ridox, Ridhox, Riducks. Could be a form of the Welsh personal name 'Rhyderch's'.

Seaside (house and estate): not a modern name, as might be expected. It has been changed to 'Riverside'.

Seven Swords, Seven Sword Handles: a field name. Could some relics of the battle of Mortimer's Cross have been found here?

Severn Field.

Shirl Heath: Old English sceran, 'Divide'. Perhaps so named because it is adjacent to the dividing line between the parishes.

Spittal Piece: site of a hospital, or land for support of one.

Staick House: Staick was formerly 'Stank', meaning 'dam'. The river was dammed here.

Stannel and Stannard: a stannard was a yard for stones.

Stytches (farm): *stich,* 'a small enclosure'. *Stitch* also means 'four sheaves of corn', but this meaning is peculiar to Devon.

Tanhouse, Tanyard: site of former tannery.

Tin Meadow.

Tippet's Brook: Tippet probably a personal name.

Twyford: double ford.

Vernall's Meadow: Vernall probably a personal name.

Wegnall, Wignall: area between the River Arrow and the mill leat. Places of this name are to be found on the Hindwell Brook, near Rodd (O.S. 323 630) and on the Pinsley between Cholestrey and Leominster (O.S. 477 595). The fact that the rivers meander considerably in these places suggests that the first element of the word refers to the wiggling or waggling of the stream. Old English *wagian* with *halh*, 'river meadow'.

Weighing House Meadow: this looks like the site of a former weighing machine.

Withy Bed: a place where osier willows grew.

Chapter Forty-Two

MISCELLANEA

The Arrow Bridge

LIKE MANY OTHER of the bridges in Herefordshire the bridge in Eardisland was sturdily rebuilt *c*. 1800 by Kingsland's famous civil engineer, John Gethin. Many of Gethin's bridges have had to be widened to accommodate the greatly increased volume of traffic. The one in Eardisland was seriously damaged during the Second World War by a convoy of American artillery. In 1945 it was widened by the County Surveyor, who avoided spoiling its appearance by using the old stones for facing and coping.

War Memorial Cross

The War Memorial Cross which stands by the Court House commemorates the dead of the Second World War. It was designed by Captain A. B. W. Greenhough, M.C., of the Staick House. The £208 which it cost was raised by public subscriptions and the land on which it stands was given by Mr. Henry Gittins of the Court House. In 1931 a collection was made to raise a sum from which the interest could be used to maintain the cross in good condition.

The Roman Occupation and Eardisland

We have already seen that Watling street, the road connecting the legionary fortresses of Caerleon and Chester, forms the eastern boundary of the parish. It crossed the Southalls Brook and the River Arrow by pitched fords at O.S. 434 587 and O.S. 434 589, the stones of which were

189

exposed and examined in 1924 by Alfred Watkins. Various objects datable to Roman times were found. Various authors state that the site of a Roman encampment was found near Burton Court, and earlier Directories of Hereford state that Twyford and Broom were occupied by the Romans. Twyford is reported to have been the regular crossing place of the River Arrow long before the Pembridge bridge was constructed.

For some years—I find mentions in 1909 and 1926— the Arrow Fishery for Trout Breeding was situated in the village.

ACKNOWLEDGEMENTS

In my search for information about Eardisland I have received help from many people to whom I here express my thanks. Chief among them is the Rev. Peter Nourse, M.A., who gave me access to the church registers and the contents of the parish chest. Others who have been generous with their help are Mrs. Pat Smith of Church Cottage, and Mr. Leslie Evans of the Brouch.

As with all the work I have done on local history, I am deeply indebted to the staffs of the City Library and the County Record Office in Hereford, and to Mr. F. C. and Miss Penelope Morgan of the Cathedral Library. Mr. W. D. Turton, solicitor of Leominster, has helped by allowing me to inspect his collection of old maps and estate plans.

INDEX

191